Jacko

The moving true story of a life rescued.

This book is of general interest, but is particularly relevant for those seeking escape from addictive lifestyles either for themselves or for those they wish to help.

Jacko

All Scripture quotations are taken from the New International Version unless otherwise stated.

Diana Rutherford can be contacted @strutherscumbernauld@gmail.com

Published by New Dawn Books 01475 729668

Contents

Foreword

I have had the privilege of knowing Jack and his wife, Jenny, for several years now.

Recently, when speaking with Jack, I discovered that I had dealings as a police officer with his previous criminal associates, who have now passed from this life. So I know what walk of life he has been rescued from. The extent to which Christ has changed both his and Jenny's lives is remarkable.

I have watched them both pass through some deep and dark waters, but their hand was held by a Saviour who walked alongside them and proved that His love for them was a love that would not let them go.

I would encourage anyone who is seeking Christ to read this down-to-earth story. I pray it will inspire many who find themself on a similar path to know that nothing can separate them from the love of God in Christ Jesus our Lord.

God bless,

Graham Rutherford

Preface

I have desired to see this story written for several years, and now it is complete. I'm not a naturally talented writer and did not find this an easy task, but I have had a God-given drive to share with the world what God can do in a soul in whom there is a fragment of hope and determination.

For the sake of privacy the names of the people have been changed, although the locations and churches remain the same.

Many thanks to my husband Graham, my son Scott, Karen Angus and Alison Black, my dear friends, for their help, support and patience in editing and proofreading.

I dedicate this book to those who suffer from the grip of addiction. May you find the kindling of hope in your hearts as you read. There is help and strength beyond your resources. Our God is the God of the impossible!

God bless.

Diana

1 The Idea

I watched from my seat at the side of the church as Jack stood behind the mic. Around seventy people were sitting in our comfortable church, listening intently to his story. The pine ceiling looked rich and warm as the sun shone through the east-facing window, and I couldn't help feeling grateful to God for all His blessings to us.

The church had started as a house group many years before when Graham and I married and moved out to Cumbernauld. We saw the blessing of God in our lives in many ways. Graham was a traffic policeman, and I was a school teacher. We had been blessed with three healthy sons who had all committed their lives to Christ and were part of the growing work of God. Over time our house group had grown steadily until, in 1997, we had this fine church built in the town, and we found ourselves ministering to a growing congregation. Many had come through the doors of the church, many had known the changing power of God in their lives, and now we were sitting listening to yet another remarkable transformation story. Jack had shared his testimony on several occasions, but he never quite got used to giving it and trembled with nerves as he stumbled through his patchy life story.

I often thought it would be good if one of our more able friends wrote his story and, on one occasion, asked somebody publicly if they would do it for me. It never quite happened, although the person seemed willing enough; other things got in the way, and so I began to think about whether I could manage to write it myself. I had mentioned it to Jack once or twice either at a house group in his home or after he had testified at church. Jack seemed keen enough.

He was a natural storyteller in a relaxed setting, such as a house group meeting. Often at the end of the evening, over a cup of tea, when the formal spiritual side was finished, Jack, with his able assistant and wife, Jenny, could keep us entertained for hours. The group of maybe eight to ten of us would be in fits of laughter as, with some persuasion, he related some of the stories of the past. Even the men among us were seen wiping their eyes from tears of laughter over his past antics. It would be only fair to say that I never heard Jack brag about his past deeds, although he would often laugh at himself over the scrapes he got into. He often had a twinkle in his eye or a mischievous grin when he told the funny stories from his past and could laugh at himself as much as anyone else did.

When I eventually retired from primary teaching at the grand old age of 59, I decided it was time to think about getting down to writing this book. It was the summer of 2020, the year of lockdown! The doors of our churches had closed during the spring of that year. Our church services had been broadcast online via Instagram.[1] These had been going well. Restrictions placed upon us made pastoral care difficult. Meeting people from other households was restricted to small groups outside only. To compensate, we invited different members to our garden for visits if the weather permitted.

---

[1] Instagram @struthers_cumbernauld

The first time Jack and Jenny visited, we had a small group of maybe eight people in the garden. It began to rain, and I still remember that as we shared the umbrellas we had gathered, Jack somehow managed to end up with my late mother's umbrella. She had passed away the previous year. It was a small ladies' tartan one, and we teased him mercilessly that his street cred was now finished! He responded laughingly, saying it had gone a long time ago. For a bit of fun, I later posted a photo of him on our church Instagram account saying, 'Jack, with Granny's brolly'! It was a lovely photo; Jack looked happy to be with us.

On his second garden visit, Government rules restricted us to meeting with only one other household, so we had Jack and Jenny over on their own. It was a gorgeous day in late summer. Jack joked, "Here I am, enjoying myself in the garden, talking with the minister!" The whole experience seemed so far removed from his past life. He mentioned he was apprehensive about coming over: what were we going to talk about, and yet here he was. He said he could not have been happier!

We discussed writing his story again. Jack seemed as happy about it as he had been earlier on. So, this time, I took responsibility for it. In lockdown and retired, I had plenty of time to think about it all.

Quite a bit of persuasion was needed when I began to chat with Jack about his life story. He would hesitate and shudder before eventually revealing some of the gory events he thought I could cope with. He never related anything distasteful, despite the fact I knew he had been involved in much violence, fought many battles, and had quite a few hidings in his life.

We finally started in November 2020 with our first Zoom call: Jack, Jenny, Graham and I chatting. Jack thought it would be easier for him if I asked him questions. So on that first occasion I just asked one question; an hour later Jack stopped and asked what the second question was! It was enough for our first session. We had recorded it so that I could play it back along with later sessions, gather information and collate it accurately. And so the writing of Jack's story began.

2 The Early Years

Jack was brought up with his younger brother George in the late 1950s in Coatbridge.[2] Their father, a rough stocky man, worked in the local steelworks, and the family home was an old single-end.[3] The boys were raised by their parents, whom they referred to as 'Mammy' and 'Da'. Their home was situated in the infamous Gartsherrie Long Row:[4] a long row of small old grey cramped houses that sat at the top of Dundyvan Steelworks. These houses were built to accommodate the workers. The family home was not a happy place; there were often many fights. The boys can't remember much about their home, apart from the fact that it was near a canal, and most, if not all, of the houses were rat-infested. From his vague memories, Jack described the old coal fire in the living room, an alcove in his parent's room with a curtain drawn across where he and George used to sleep, and an outside toilet. He remembers the old stairwell leading to the house and Mammy going down to the washhouses where the women washed their

---

[2] Coatbridge was once known as the 'Iron Burgh' because of its many ironworks. It lies eight and a half miles east of Glasgow in North Lanarkshire, in the central lowlands, and has strong links with Lanarkshire's industrial heritage. http://www.visitlanarkshire.com/explore/coatbridge/

[3] Single-end – a one-roomed flat or house.

[4] 'Gartsherrie Long Rows were built in the 1800s to house employees of Gartsherrie Ironworks and their families. They lacked basic modern amenities and were demolished to make way for modern housing in the 1960s. www.culturenlmuseums.co.uk/SIMode/Detail/11564

clothes and put them through the old wringers. She would often go down to the 'Slap Up'[5] nearby.

The two young boys can remember their parents fighting. Some of their earliest unhappy memories were of being woken during the night by their poor mother screaming. From their bed, as they peeped their heads through the curtain covering the alcove, the two little boys could see that Da was pulling Mammy about by the hair. As a result, these little ones were terrified; they didn't understand what was happening and lived in constant fear waiting for further incidents. Da had always been violent and for as long as Jack could remember, there were problems in the home.

One day the boys were playing in the cul-de-sac outside their Auntie's house whilst Mammy had been visiting her sister. It was a grey, dreary day and the brothers had been left to play outside on the street. Suddenly, Mammy came down the close[6] stairs, and after chatting with her sister, she just waved to the boys and walked quickly away. Jack and his brother stood watching her,

---

[5] 'Slap Up' - an infamous area of Coatbridge, off Dundyvan Road, consisting of Kirk Street, Turner Street, Henderson Street and Douglas Street. It got its nickname because the stone-built tenements were reputedly 'slapped up' in 60 days, sometime during the first decade of the 20th Century.' By the early 1960s, much of the 'Slap Up' was in a dilapidated state and the area was soon to be redeveloped. www.google.co.uk/search?q=slap.up+coatbridge+history&ie=UTF-8&oe=UTF-8&hl=en-gb&client=safari Lanarkshire Family History Society Facebook.

[6] Close – the entry to a tenement house, the open passageway giving access to the common stairs and the flats on the floors above.

wondering where she was going, as she called back over her shoulder, "I'll be back in an hour." They didn't understand what was happening, but they did not see their mother again for two years!

That fateful grey afternoon, little Jack and George's world was turned upside down. The two boys ended up being taken into Care that night. Jack was confused. He looks back and remembers being taken to the children's home by his Da. He had no idea where his Mammy had gone, why she had not come home, and why now he had been taken into a strange place he had never been in before. A vivid memory remains with him, over the long years, of walking in through the big door that day, climbing the massive stairwell and being put to bed by a stranger whilst his little brother George was put into a cot some distance away. Jack said, "I was seven, he was five, and we got separated. From that day, all through my life, I've felt awfully protective of ma George". Jack and his brother lived in the children's home for two years.

After the chaos of their family life, the discipline of the children's home felt very harsh. This mansion had large rooms with high ceilings. The unfamiliar surroundings where the boys were separated from each other made life feel strange after the cramped conditions they had lived in. The rigorous routines of meals and bedtimes, the constant noise and clamour of others, the lack of their familiar mother's presence and, on occasion, abusive treatment the boys tolerated made the children's home a dark period in their childhood. Jack explained that he and his brother blanked out many unhappy memories from their time in Care, and things that happened there were never discussed later. There were times when inappropriate and abusive incidents took place. Jack did not wish to say more than that. The boys never talked about these matters, not even in later life when they were both under the influence of drink and drugs. There was only one time Jack remembers when George turned to him and said, "That was wrong what happened to us then, wasn't it? Jack said, "Aye," and it was never mentioned again.

After Mammy disappeared, Da returned to live with his own family. Da's parents had died when he was young. Instead, he had been brought up by a couple whom Jack can remember calling 'Nanny' and 'Pappy', although they were not his biological grandparents. When the boys were taken into care, they were allowed to visit Da weekly at Nanny and Pappy's house. Jack's earliest memories are of the anger and hate vented by his grandparents towards his Mammy. He was told repeatedly, "If you see your mother spit on her!" Again and again, this was drummed into the boys. Jack didn't understand what his Mammy had done, although as time went by, the picture became clear.

As these visits continued, Jack kept hearing the name of a man being spoken in a derogatory manner by his grandparents. Even as a young boy, he began to understand that his mum had left him to run off with this other man. The adults in the family didn't seem to think about sparing the boys this upsetting information; they only wanted the boys to hate her. They didn't understand that in the poor woman's attempt to find peace, she had run away with one of Da's friends. Mammy's unfaithfulness had broken Da. He never forgave her, and he never recovered. Years later, Mammy did come home, and the family were together again, but things were just the same, and after a drinking session, Da would become angry, cursing and swearing as he brought up this man's name. These chaotic scenes ended in horrible violence as Da lifted his hand repeatedly to the boy's mother. Jack learned to hate the very mention of this other man's name. Sometime later Da and his brothers, as violent as he, dealt with the man involved in the affair. Jack never described what his father and uncles did, but the three brothers were imprisoned for a time!

As the children's home was in a different locality, Jack had to move to another primary school and found he had a hard time. A special bus was arranged for the children from the Home to take them to this new school. Children can be cruel, and he can remember being taunted because he was from the Home. He got into constant trouble for fighting; this became a pattern of his behaviour later.

Jack attended school in the 1960s. At that time it was the custom for a teacher to be in the playground, carrying around a bell during playtime, and she would ring it by hand when playtime was over. Jack can remember that at one of these playtimes, the teacher in charge approached the two brothers to let them know their mother was just outside the school. They looked over to where the teacher had pointed, and there she was, peering through the railings at them. Immediately they ran over to see her. They could not believe it! Suddenly a huge commotion broke out outside the school: Da had appeared from nowhere, and he was angry! Right in front of the boys, he pulled Mammy away from the school, disappearing into a nearby close with her. Jack had been so pleased to see her and was now disappointed and frightened by his Da's reactions. He doesn't remember seeing her again for some time. However, a secret hope grew inside him: Mammy was back in Coatbridge.

These two small boys had such a mixed-up childhood that they never knew how long they were in the Home. Jack used to try and join the memories together as he grew up. They were like pieces of a jigsaw that floated through his mind. When he asked his parents questions later in life about his early childhood, rows would often break out in the family home as if he was touching a sore point. He was told that he and George were only in the children's home for six weeks, but Jack can remember more. "My mammy told me I'd been in the Home for six weeks, but I knew that I was in there for more! There was a big playroom with red and cream tiles on the floor. I can remember it vividly. At Christmas time you got a pillow slip with your name on it. I can remember getting more than one pillow slip, so I was in for more than one Christmas."

After the boys had spent two years in the Home, their parents were allowed to take them back to the family home. Both parents had had to attend some form of marriage guidance counselling to help them at least give the appearance of stability, but from Jack's point of view, things only got worse rather than better. The boys not only had to cope with returning to an unhappy home life, but they also had the disruption of moving schools again. It was after this time that the family grew, and Jack and George became brothers to two younger sisters. These girls were spared the worst of the family troubles, and although they saw the difficulties between Jack and his father, they never fully understood the problem.

Several years after the boys had moved back home with their parents, the family relocated to a new housing scheme: the brand-new flats at Sykeside. The infamous Long Row of single ends was being demolished. Not only did the boys move house, but about ten or eleven of the Long Row families also moved over to the new scheme, the posh electric flats as they were called because they had electric heating.

Other families began to move into this new scheme, which became the shortest-lived housing scheme in Scotland. These families came from many different areas, and as they began to mix, trouble soon followed, which led to a police station being built right in the centre of the scheme! By this time, Jack would have been about twelve years old. As the youngsters got to know each other, he remembered some good and some rough times.

However, despite the new surroundings, hearts remained the same. Many fathers were similar: they drank heavily and were prone to violent tendencies. Things didn't change much at home. Every time there was a row, Da would take it out on the boys and their mother. Jack said that Da would get hold of a belt and whack them "until the urine was flying out of you!".

As he got older, he found he was constantly angry inside. Resentment and bitterness continually gnawed at him: none of his relatives had bothered with the two boys and taken them in but had allowed them to go into Care. That was the pattern of his life; no one had been interested in him. It was a pain that often surfaced when he had been drinking; memories became twisted, twisting Jack in the process.

Jack finally found out the truth about his childhood later in life. Two things happened that helped him to piece together his past. In his forties, he was laying slabs at a big house in Coatbridge. He said, "As I walked into the house, suddenly memories came flooding back of the old, huge stairwell at the front door and the red and cream tiles in the playroom." This large house was the very home Jack had been in for two years with so many unhappy memories. He wanted to find out the rest of the story and fit these disjointed memories together, so one day it bothered him enough to do something about it. He visited the primary school he had attended when living in the children's home. As he drove into the car park, he made up his mind to invent some story from his past and ask the secretary to check through written records to see how long he had been at the school. She was happy to oblige, and after checking records, she phoned him three days later, confirming that both boys had been there for two years, as Jack had suspected. He was angry at being deceived and took it out on his parents.

Over the years, Mammy never forgave herself for leaving the children. As Jack grew older, he understood that his poor mother did not want to go into her past. She fobbed him off, again and again evading the truth, saying she had only been away for six weeks. Towards the end of his life, Da developed Alzheimer's disease, and she used to treat him like a baby when caring for him. It was as if she was trying to make up for her wrong choices. She used to cry in bed every night, asking God to forgive her. This poor woman carried her guilt until she died. One day, when Mammy was near the end, she and Jack were alone. She asked Jack if he would forgive her for these early years. As he sat with her, she explained how violent his father had been. It slowly began to dawn on him just how she must have felt. He realised the terrible violence she faced and how frightened she must have been: she had no choice but to get out of the situation. Mammy might have made some terrible mistakes, but she still loved her boys and ultimately paid the price to be with them. Jack loved his mother dearly and, with a very willing heart, reassured her that all was forgiven and most forgotten.

3 Teenage Years

Jack soon got to know a large crowd of boys who hung around together in gangs. Some of the boys were older than Jack, and they got up to all sorts of mischief, causing havoc on the streets of the new housing scheme. They played games and committed little misdemeanours, for example, 'chap door run away' and smashing all the little windows of the old gas street lamps. As the boys grew older, the pranks and misconduct became more serious, and getting chased by the police became a regular occurrence. In those days the police drove about in old Bedford vans. One of their favourite pranks was rocking the police vans right over, although thankfully the vans were empty! Jack remembers the fun of making bogie carts out of bits of old wood and pram wheels and racing them downhill. Despite the boyish pranks and rival friendships that developed, things were still unhappy when Jack returned home at night, and he often clashed with his Da.

One night Jack had been out smoking with his friends. His Mammy was at work, and when Jack came home Da smelt the smoke from his clothes. He asked Jack if he had been smoking and immediately began to belt him. Jack shuddered as he recalled the incident, "Honestly, he nearly killed me, I mean badly." The following day, after being beaten up by his Da, he went to see the doctor with a suspected broken jaw and a pair of sunglasses on to hide the bruising. He remembers making some excuse about being 'jumped' by a gang. Although the visit to the Doctor was unusual, the violence was not. Da often used the boys as a punching bag. Jack can still remember his Da pulling his hair to inflict pain.

Da also encouraged the boys to be aggressive towards Catholics. Feelings between Catholics and Protestants have always been antagonistic in central Scotland, and Da was a bigot and strongly connected with the annual Orange walks. In July, the loyalists used to arrive from Northern Ireland and the boys were taken along to the 'All Blue' nights at the local Orange Hall. The boys can remember the bowler hats and the sashes, the heavy drinking frequently followed by trouble. It was drummed into them both from the early years that they should only marry a Protestant. When invited to a Catholic wedding, Jack would either refuse to go into the chapel or sit awkwardly at the back. He had been taught not to agree with or believe in Catholicism but to hate it.

By the time Jack was thirteen years old, he was hanging around regularly with a gang from the local area whilst rival gangs formed from other districts around Coatbridge. Recognising the growing problem amongst young people, churches and chapels opened their doors for social purposes. They used their adjacent church halls for non-alcoholic discos for young folks to help with the social problems that had developed in the area. The boys used to go together as a gang, dressed in the same dress code: Crombie coats and big bovver[7] boots. Other rival gangs would come to their patch, and, in turn, Jack and his crowd would go to their areas. Fights were frequent amongst the lads. Jack can remember feeling out of his depth when going into a different locality where brawls developed and escalated into serious trouble. The police were often around and began to get to know the

---

[7] Stout lace-up boots, often with a steel toecap, perceived to be worn to kick people in fights.

local hooligans from the various housing schemes. Fortunately, the drug world had not opened amongst the youths, and although some of Jack's friends would drink cheap wine, Jack never touched it.

Violence continued inside the home. Jack explained, "Da's enormous hands would close into a fist and hit us hard. He never used a weapon; he never had to, his fist was enough!' As a result, Jack became increasingly volatile outside the home. If anyone from the gang touched him, he discovered he would explode into rage. Other lads learned to watch their step with him. His anger and rebellion continued, and he grew increasingly aggressive. Jack took so much physical pain that he realised it could not hurt him anymore; he grew immune to it. He learned to develop a frame of mind that said he did not care. He said, "I got used to the beatings and the belt."

By the time he was fourteen, he was a rebel without a cause: he couldn't cope with school, and school couldn't cope with him. He was always waiting outside the 'Beak's'[8] office for one reason or another. Jack remembered a particular teacher in school who hated him and would always give him the belt. One day, he decided it was payback time. This teacher led the brass band, and it was his pride and joy to conduct them every Friday afternoon at the whole school assembly. So, before the school assembly that particular week, he, along with a couple of his friends, went around every member of the brass band and told them that they were

---

[8] Nickname for the Headmaster of the school.

dogging[9] school on Friday. Sure enough, when it was time for the assembly, Jack took them all down the glen, and not one member of the brass band turned up that day for the Friday assembly. The teacher in question was furious! The following week, each member of the brass band had to report to the 'Beak' to explain their absence, and of course, each one, in turn, blamed Jack for their disappearance. So, Jack was in further trouble! He always maintained he wasn't a bully, but he was aware that day he had pushed the boat out too far with these music students! In those days, the legal maximum of six lashes of the belt in one go was in place. This particular teacher used to ensure that the tails of the belt would strike the pupil's wrist. This could be painful, leaving welts. One day at school, Jack was in trouble as usual; he was taken out of the class by the same teacher and was given six lashes of the belt. He cannot remember what happened that particular day, but he knows that when he returned to the classroom, he made some cheeky comments to the teacher. The class gasped in horror, and the teacher, mad with rage, marched Jack back out of the classroom to give him a second six of the belt! Jack had had enough. He grabbed the belt from the teacher and wrapped it around the teacher's neck before shooting off downstairs along a spiral staircase, forbidden to pupils. Jack ran to the 'Beak's' office to explain the situation before the teacher arrived. Unfortunately, he was too late! The teacher had got there first, and Jack was in for further punishment.

Jack explained that he could not win. When he was suspended from school, he used to pretend to his

---

[9] Slang for skipping school.

parents that he was at school. When he had no school to go to, he could be outside in all weathers all day. His Da used to threaten to 'batter' him if he was late home or soaking wet after being out in the rain. In Jack's mind, there was no escape in any direction. He had his Da to deal with, teachers to contend with, and the Beak at the end of it all! So, in his mind, he just thought, "Yahoo! I might as well go for it!" There were no limits or restrictions: Jack was out of control, and eventually, after one final prank, he was expelled from school and ran away to his uncle. His name was Arthur, one of Da's brothers who had moved south to Leeds; he had a reputation for throwing his weight about. It was to this uncle that Jack went when home life became unbearable and school was no longer a possibility. He was Jack's hero: the one he went to if he was in serious difficulty. Arthur treated him well and spoke to him like a man.

The final prank happened one day whilst in the school library. He and his friend spotted the teacher's bag under her desk. They planned and then staged a fight right in front of her desk to steal money from the teacher's purse! After a pretend skirmish on the floor, Jack stole a five-pound note from the lady's purse and then, to their dismay, they heard the 'Beak' coming along the corridor. He had a very distinctive walk as he had a wooden leg and could be heard some distance away. Jack quickly hid the money inside a library book just before the 'Beak' came in. Within a few minutes, Jack was pinned on the ground by the 'Beak' before being hauled to his feet and marched to his office. The two boys were thrown out of school in disgrace with the threat that the police would be along that evening to see their fathers. The money was found later that week by one of Jenny's best friends,

Eileen, who came across it out of the thousands of books in the library! She gave it back to the library teacher concerned.

Jack was too frightened to face an angry Da once again, so he raced home whilst his Da was still at work, packed a bag, and then he and his friend sought shelter that night in a semi-built house on a building site in Bellshill. In the morning the runaways, not wanting to go home, stood at the side of the road and hitched a lift which took them to Carlisle. Jack was running away south to Uncle Arthur! By the time the boys arrived in Carlisle, they were hungry, so they stole a bottle of milk that was sitting on the doorstep of the local police house! It wasn't long before two policemen picked the boys up, took them back to the police station and contacted their parents. The boys' dads had to take time off work, hire a car, and drive over 100 miles to pick them up. Jack can still remember sitting in Carlisle Police Station. As his Da entered the police station, he caught sight of Jack and ran at him in a rage. The police had to hold him back from assaulting his son. After things calmed down, the fathers took the boys home again. It wasn't a happy car journey home! Jack can remember his mate being in the front of the hired car whilst his father demanded to know what had happened. Poor Jack was stuck in the back with his own Da and got whacked for the whole journey back home to Scotland! When they were back, the boys stood before a juvenile court, and Jack was remanded in custody in Blantyre at a place called Calder House, where he was given three weeks of confinement. In those days, it was called Borstal.

Calder House was very disciplined. Boys slept in dormitories, and Jack's memory was of a regimented timetable of education, football, and cleaning, including being responsible for his laundry. Jack said it was just like being in prison. If the boys did something wrong or didn't pay attention in lessons, the old warden would throw his keys at them. They were allowed occasional visits from their families. Most of the boys smoked; the fathers had to sign papers to let the boys smoke five cigarettes a day. Jack's Da refused to sign. When he came to visit Jack, he just belted him! After three weeks, Jack got released from Calder House, and on returning home, his parents decided to give him one more chance.

Things did not change for Jack. He was still the same angry, frustrated young man and now out of control. He was getting into serious trouble running wild with the gangs who used steel combs to slash people's faces. He found himself appearing regularly in the local police station, and before long he began to appear frequently before juvenile courts too. He didn't care about his Da anymore. After being in trouble with the police, he would walk into the house and think, "Here it comes!" as his Da rushed at him in rage. He learned to protect his head and just took the abuse. Jack discovered that anger and hatred escalated within himself, so whenever he was threatened, the explosion of anger raged inside him again and again. He said, "I would have fought with ma shadow because I took so much off my Da; physical pain couldn't hurt anymore."

Most of the trouble at home lay between the sons and their father. His sisters never knew all that lay between Da and the two brothers. They never knew about the children's home, and Jack never felt inclined to tell them, but they saw and heard the continual aggression. Jack persisted in questioning why he was put into Care. It troubled him, he had such unhappy memories and felt so let down by his parents, but his Da would 'leather' him when he talked about it. As he got older, he learned to hit back. When he knew trouble was brewing, Jack would put his boots on; he was ready to kick hard. Although he got more hidings than he would have liked, he learned to stand up to his father. His sisters would ask, "How do you not like our Da?" but Jack never told them. They heard bits and pieces, but he could never sit down and explain how he felt. He told me, "I wouldn't be selfish enough to run my Daddy down. My sisters used to worship him." He felt pushed aside by his parents as if that part of life did not exist. Family relationships never improved between them right up to the end of Da's life; the two men never reconciled.

In contrast, Jack always felt respected and safe in the company of his Uncle Arthur, who carried a gangster aura. He was always there for Jack, no matter what he had done. In his late teens and even as a married man, whenever Jack hit a problem or when trouble followed him, he used to run away from his difficulties by hopping on the bus and off he would go down south to his Uncle Arthur. The two men in Jack's life were very different from each other. His father had an abusive way of speaking to him, whereas his uncle appeared to listen to Jack, and their relationship seemed better, at least it did in Jack's eyes. Arthur's way of coping with his young, troubled nephew was to introduce him to more trouble! Arthur demanded money with menaces in all the local pubs he visited. Jack can remember going around the pubs with him. He sensed the respect folks had for his uncle. On one occasion, Jack remembered a publican handed Arthur and his associate a big bundle of notes. Jack often wondered what this was all about not realising that these men demanded money to protect their pubs. If there were difficulties, Arthur would deal with it, he kept the pubs quiet, and if they did not pay him, there would be consequences too! On reflection, Jack realised that Arthur was a man who had just run away from his troubles. He had a lot of street cred and took time to train Jack to deal with people on the street.

4 The Romance

When Jack was in his mid-teens, he became involved with Jenny, the girl who would become his future wife. It was one of the best things that happened to Jack as a young man; the relationship helped steady him, at least for a time.

Jenny and Jack first met in primary school, although Jack had little recollection of her then. The girls and boys had separate playgrounds and went into school by different entrances. Jenny can remember that the boys used to peer at the girls through the playground bars, and she can distinctly remember thinking she did not like Jack because he had a big scar on his face. As the two children attended school, Jenny can remember body-swerving him. In her own words, "He was intimidating, and he stole my duffle coat!" she laughed. According to Jack, if you owned a duffle coat, it got stolen and sold.

Jack first noticed Jenny at high school. As he stood outside the Beak's office waiting for some form of punishment, he saw Jenny walking past with her shiny prefect's badge gleaming on her smart prefect's blazer! He described her as being Miss Goody-Two-Shoes! It was obvious she came from a good home. Jack didn't like her; he thought she was a snob. They were both brought up in the same school and town, but their worlds were very far apart.

One day Jack and his pal were out selling fake football scratch cards. They always knew who the winner was as they would peel the stickers back to check before selling them, and then they would go around and collect their winnings. They were knocking at front doors and soon found themselves at Jenny's door. She bought one. That was the first time Jack and Jenny had spoken, and somehow, word got back to Jack that Jenny liked him. There was something in Jack's wild nature that appealed to her, and that was it. He didn't need any further encouragement before he asked her out. On their first date, Jack took her to a 'card school', held in a close, with all his unruly mates! Jack can remember getting dressed up for the occasion - donning the Crombie coat and the bovver boots, and off he went to collect her. Jenny was pleased to see him but very unnerved, leaving her familiar streets. She visited an area that had an undesirable reputation and found herself amongst a group of youths she did not know. She stood nervously at the side, watching the boys playing cards and did not join in. The girls that Jack knew were rough and ready, not like Jenny, who had been brought up in a better area. They were not always very nice to new girls coming in from outwith their circles and often used to make fun of them. Jenny can remember one night being at a dance with Jack. She went to the ladies' room, and the same group came around her, standing in a semi-circle, taunting and mocking her. She was petrified and told Jack about it later; one word from him and they never bothered her again.

Jack and Jenny lived only an eight- or nine-minute walk away from each other, but they were from two districts that were very different. For Jenny, it was a whole new world going into this crazy housing scheme, and it was a new world for Jack, going into Jenny's Mammy and Daddy's house! Jenny's dad was a works manager, a no-nonsense kind of man. Jack found it very awkward just sitting and talking in the living room, being asked how he was doing, and having a cup of tea with a biscuit. To him, this all seemed very abnormal. As Jack said, "My house was in total chaos all the time!" Jenny must have known he was different. She lived in peace, and Jack in chaos.

Jenny's daddy was a strict man and took good care of his daughter. It took him a long time to get used to the idea that Jenny was going out with Jack, who by this time was known in the local area as 'Jacko' and had a bit of a reputation. Around eleven pm when Jack was visiting Jenny at home, her dad would get up and start putting the lights out and say, 'Right, it's time to go home!' There was no nonsense! Jack had to leave.

As soon as Jack met Jenny, he began to pull away from the gang. He had found something better and, for the first time, was discovering a new way of life which he liked. He started to quieten down and, at the grand age of fifteen, for the first time, began thinking about settling down. Jack tried to speak to his old friends and explain that he was finished running about with them. He had quietened down and met a girl; he asked them not to bother him.

On one occasion, just shortly after they had been going out, Jenny decided to go skating with another lad from one of the rival gangs from Kirkshaws. Jack was having none of this! No one was taking his girl away! So, despite the skating rink being outside his local neighbourhood, Jack took the risk of crossing into different territory and set off to get her back. It was an unspoken rule, amongst the guys at least, that girls could go anywhere whilst guys were only welcome on their home turf. Arriving at the ice rink, he hired a pair of skates and kept an eye out for Jenny. As he fastened the skates, he leaned against a wall to help him keep his balance when Jenny's new boyfriend skated past, deliberately clipping Jack on the elbow. Jack lost his balance and fell to the ground, finally ending up at the hospital with a broken arm. Poor Jack! He reappeared with a stookie![10] Several years later, he found out where the guy worked, and shall we say he got his own back!

After this incident, the new couple went everywhere together. They fell madly in love and could not wait to see each other. Saturday was their special day out, and they would take a train into Glasgow to spend the day there. One day when they were on their way home on a train, two guys entered the carriage they were in. They were covered in blood. Jack knew them both as they were from a rival gang. Immediately recognising Jack, they called to him, explaining that one of Jack's friends had slashed one of their mates. The lads were only sixteen, but Jack sensed things were getting out of hand.

This confirmed again to Jack that he was doing the right thing by pulling away from his old life. He did not want any more trouble as he had found something much better and, for the first time, was much happier. He would walk Jenny home at night, body-swerving the boys, and they left him alone, recognising he was now involved with a girl. Sometimes he babysat with Jenny on a Saturday night, or they would go to the pictures together. Jack felt that he and Jenny were made for one another. He could not have done better; Jenny was made for him, and in his

---

[10] Scots slang for a plaster-cast.

own words, "I didn't kick a ball out of place!" There was no arguing or fighting, and he never touched a drop of alcohol, even though his peers were all drinking by this time.

At one point, not long after he had been going out with Jenny, Jack decided to try for a position in the Royal Navy. He saw an advert for a training opportunity in the catering department, training for silver service, and thought it would be fun to work on cruise liners. His application was successful, and Jack began to prepare to leave home and move south to Gravesend. Jenny and Da took him to Central Station in Glasgow to see him off. Da was making sure Jack got on the train! Jack met another lad going on the same thirteen-week course. The lads became good friends as they travelled south together and, before too long, were working hard on board the ship, finding they fitted in very well to this new environment. Other lads seemed young and immature and were upset about leaving their families, whilst Jack was glad to be away from his! He liked the discipline, the independence, and the new challenges the course afforded him. If he had not met Jenny, Jack reckons he would have enjoyed the job and been retired by now, probably somewhere abroad, but his heartstrings were pulling him, and after only one phone call to Jenny, Jack decided to pack his bags and travel back home. The romance was more important.

Thankfully, after Jack came home, he got a job that he enjoyed as an apprentice with the local blacksmith, and discovered to his satisfaction that he not only enjoyed it but was very good at it. One day, when chatting with a guy who lived in the same block of flats, he told him about his apprenticeship. The guy was very interested, and Jack encouraged him to apply for a job as an apprentice blacksmith with the same company. He was successful, and the two men became friends. One morning as they were on their way to work together, his friend turned to Jack and told him he was in trouble. Jack asked him what the problem was, and he explained that an incident had happened only the night before. There had been a group of six boys hanging about together. Thankfully, Jack had not been with them as he had been out with Jenny. The boys had thrown a large stone at a car as it drove past and smashed the windshield. As if this was not bad enough, the driver had been seriously injured, and an ambulance had to be called. On that same day at work, men arrived in suits. It was the CID, and they arrested the young man who worked with Jack. All six of the lads ended up with a hefty sentence and imprisonment. Unfortunately, the poor gentleman in the car had a severe brain injury. Jack was relieved he was now in tow with Jenny.

He would often stop off at Jenny's house as he walked home from work, and Jenny would come out of the house and meet him at the end of her garden path for a blether.[11] The relationship had been blossoming for two or three years when one day at the garden gate Jenny asked Jack to marry her! Jack's romantic response was, "You're joking! What do you mean you want to get married?" Jenny had it all worked out! Her dad, known between them as 'Jo Millionaire', would give them the money, and they would get married and go on their honeymoon. The young couple became excited about

---

[11] Scots slang for a talk.

their hopes and shared their ideas with Jenny's parents. They agreed to the plan, and the youngsters were delighted and began to prepare for their wedding.

Jenny was very keen to get married in a church. Although her family were not churchgoers, she had been sent to Sunday School as a little girl. The young couple went to speak to the local minister about getting married. He questioned them carefully as to why they had chosen his church. Jenny explained that he had been their school chaplain, and this was the church she had attended as a young child. During the interview, Jack slowly realised that this man, the minister, was the husband of the lady that Jack had robbed of five pounds in the school library! Nothing was said about the incident at the time, but after discussing it with Jenny, they were sure the minister knew who Jack was! However, whether the minister overlooked the incident or not, he seemed satisfied with their answers, and so a date was fixed, and a big wedding was laid on at the local church for the young couple. Jack was eighteen and Jenny only sweet seventeen when they took their vows and made their promises to one another. Their planned honeymoon followed in Blackpool with half of Jenny's family in tow! Jack added to his story, "I've got to say this, we didn't have to get married. There was no wee Steven on the way; he came later. We just wanted to be together."

Jenny's dad was a good influence on Jack, and he realised his bigoted upbringing was wrong. He decided to reject it all and change his attitude towards Catholics. Looking back at his Da after he died, he said, "I'm going to be honest. I felt sorry for him. He was just an angry, twisted, bitter man. Whoever was in his road when he went 'aff on one',[12] he took it out on them."

Jack now had a better influence in his life and had every opportunity of making the right choices. The young couple moved in with Jenny's parents and began their married life. He looks back now, knowing God had brought him and Jenny together.

---

[12] Scots slang for off on a drinking session.

5 Apprenticeship and Addiction

If only life could have remained as happy as it had been for the young couple! But before too long, Jack began to go down the compelling road of addiction.

Jack loved his job working at the blacksmith's. Often he would work long, hard hours and then come home to Jenny at the end of the day. At that time, they lived in Jenny's parents' home as they couldn't afford a place to live.

One evening after a busy week at work, Jack's boss offered to take him out for a drink. Jack had made a point of never touching a drop of alcohol during his gang days. He was now nineteen years old. However, this night was different; perhaps it was the influence of his boss. Jack can still remember, as he accepted the offer, took the pint in his hand and gulped down the liquor, the sensation of the warm glow it gave him. He felt a sense of relief and security and, boy, did he feel good! If he had only known where this would lead, he might have been more careful, but it was the beginning of a long dark road for the young couple.

Within a year of married bliss, Jack began to drink heavily, and changes began to come over him. He worked five days a week and, on top of that, did two late nights on a Tuesday and a Thursday. He got into the habit of going straight from work to the pub with the guys, and that is when it all began to go downhill for him. Jack would have been home for his dinner at 7:30 pm on an ordinary night, but instead, he was coming in at 10:30 pm, more than a little drunk. The young couple began to argue, and Jenny's mum and dad listened to the arguments from downstairs. Eventually, Jack would stay out all night. Their marriage lasted only two or three months in Jenny's parents' house before Jack was thrown out! When things improved and Jack apologised, Jenny forgave him, and he would return home again. But before too long, it all began again, and he was repeatedly kicked out. This kind of behaviour went on for two years. Jenny's dad couldn't believe the change that had come over Jack so quickly. He appeared a responsible young man at the beginning, and now he was not even coming home at night! Jack admits that when he was doing stupid things in their early married days, Jenny's dad made him feel like a 'mass murderer'! Sometimes he would go to someone else's house with the guys he worked with and drink there. He would occasionally wake up in the morning in a different home, not knowing how he got there and often went straight to work in a state. This young, promising apprentice was throwing his life away so quickly. His manager had given Jack glowing reports up to that point, and now he was so concerned that he arranged to meet with Jenny and her mum. He was puzzled by Jack's sudden drinking habits. He wanted to know if there was anything causing problems at home that explained his behaviour. In a short space of time, drinking had become a total addiction. The company let Jack finish his apprenticeship, and then they reluctantly got rid of him. Jenny can remember them saying to her, "We wish you all the best of luck with him."

Amid all these difficulties, Jenny fell pregnant with their first-born son Steven. After the baby was born, the young couple was offered a council house. Jenny and Jack decided as young parents, both still in their late teens, that they would make a new go of things and gladly took up the offer from the council. Jenny's father came down and helped decorate the house, making it look lovely for them. Despite the new home and the new start, Jack's drinking was so heavy that the couple only lasted six weeks together. Jack came home from work one day to find the house had been emptied. He said with a rueful smile, "All that was left was a cabinet and a candle sitting on it." Jenny and her family had had enough at that point! However, over the years, the young couple kept getting back together again and again. It was hardly any wonder that it took Jenny's family between twelve to fourteen years to accept Jack into their family! He brought so much trouble. Sadly, Jack continued to spend long hours out drinking with his buddies, and when he did come home, he did not take any responsibility as a father to his young son or as a husband to his young wife. Jack admitted there was nothing nasty going on; he was not being unfaithful to his wife; he was only drinking, sitting around in his working clothes, lying down wherever he could find a place to rest, sometimes even at his Mammy's house instead of coming home to his family.

Things eventually became difficult between the young couple, so they sought advice regarding a divorce, and arrangements were made for Jack to have his young son every Saturday. When they were only three weeks from a divorce settlement, Jack went, as usual, to collect baby Steven from Jenny's parents. The young couple had not been on speaking terms for some time, but on arriving at the house on this occasion, Jack courteously asked how Jenny was managing, and it was just enough to melt a chink in her hardened sore heart. She commented that she was doing okay, but there was one thing that she did not have that she would like. Jack went home puzzled, wondering what she meant. Around this time, Jack had got to know another blacksmith from Bellshill. The two men became friends and soon discovered that they had much in common between their drinking habits and unstable marriages, and before long, Jack had moved into his flat. The Bellshill friend was in the same position where his marriage was on and off, although eventually his wife returned home.

As Jack pondered Jenny's comment, he realised she had been speaking about wanting Jack back in her life, so he gave her a phone call, and Jenny agreed to meet up with him. The couple decided at the eleventh hour to try and give things another go. After all, they still loved each other even though it had been a rocky start. Arrangements were soon made for a friend of Jack's to pick Jenny up and bring her over to his new digs. Jenny's Mum and Dad were wild about this decision! Their beloved daughter and first grandson were getting into a car with a stranger. She was going back to her irresponsible drunken husband, and she had a young baby in tow. At that point, they washed their hands off her. She was no longer welcome home again.

Whether it was the pressure of having nowhere else to go or not, the young couple managed to live together for a whole year in the Bellshill flat before moving south of the border to a new job in Newcastle, England.

6. From Newcastle to South Africa

Jack, who was by now in his early twenties, was one day wandering past the Job Centre in Bellshill when he spotted an advert for a job as a blacksmith in Newcastle. He had, after all, completed his apprenticeship, and he thought this might be a new beginning for him, so he applied for the job and was successful. Jack and Jenny made arrangements to move south and soon found a house. They hoped for a clean break and the beginning of better things.

Despite Jack's attempts at a new beginning, he found that his addiction followed him. He used to work twelve-hour shifts and then go straight into the clubs in Newcastle. He discovered that the Geordies loved their drink as much as he did. He settled into the pattern of drinking in the pub all evening, arriving home late to go to bed and then up and away in the morning, back to work. This continued until, eventually, the firm intervened. His addictive lifestyle was taking its toll on his performance. The manager arranged for him to be on a permanent night shift, hoping it would break his drinking cycle. There were another three guys in his squad, so to begin with, Jack didn't drink, as they kept an eye on him, but then he found a way around the system. Eventually he began smuggling drink into his work. Not only was he drinking on the job, but Jack also got a back injury.

One day when working with a steam hammer, he twisted awkwardly. Perhaps the constant pressure on his back weakened something, but Jack found himself in continuous pain from that time on. He was also facing uncertain times at home. He and Jenny really did love each other, but the lonely young mother could not cope with the long days on her own with a tiny baby and eventually decided to move back to Coatbridge. They were not splitting up this time. Jenny enquired about getting a house in Coatbridge, and when a home became available she moved up north again. She kept in touch with Jack by telephone, and although he stayed on for another couple of months, he eventually returned home. The young couple settled in Coatbridge for about a year and a half before their next adventure.

During that period, Jack was suffering from painful spasms in his back. After attending the doctor, he was referred to the hospital, where he was given traction three or four times. In the end, the medics decided they had to operate. It was a delicate, difficult and dangerous operation; the surgeon worked very near Jack's spinal cord. If it had gone wrong, it would have led to paralysis. Jack was in the hospital for eight months after a long twelve-hour operation, and it took some time before he was mobile again. To help him cope with the pain, the doctor put him on Temazepam, which badly affected Jack's mood swings. He seemed a changed person on these tablets. So, with some encouragement from Jenny, he returned to the doctor, and the medication was changed to Diazepam. Three months later, Jack discovered he was hooked! It was twenty-five years later before he managed to break the cycle of the addiction that started at that time. Jack explained it was worse than coming off heroin. He described it as "hell on earth!"

Life seemed to be destroying the young couple no matter how hard they tried to make things work. Jenny was a home bird whilst Jack, living recklessly, found himself, again and again, waking up in his Mammy's house or some other friend's home after heavy drinking sessions. Eventually, the couple decided, once again, to try and change their way of life. Jenny's sister was living in South Africa at the time. She and Jenny often spoke to one another on the phone, and she encouraged Jenny and Jack to move out to join her and her husband. She told Jack about all the available job opportunities where she lived. Far-distant horizons of work, warmth and wealth attracted the young couple, so they made plans to cross the continents. This involved considerable planning as Jenny was now expecting their second child. She moved back home to her parents whilst twenty-four-year-old Jack packed up and got ready to leave the country. He was always looking for dodges: getting loans and then not paying them back, and he did just that on this occasion. He left his house, his wife, his young family and all the debts he owed and got a one-way ticket, an Apex,[13] to sunnier climes. The plan was that Jenny would join him later when he had found work.

Jack arrived in South Africa and soon realised that the horizon was not quite as bright as he had hoped, as there were no jobs. He was in a jam! His pregnant wife and young child were thousands of miles away whilst he was here, in South Africa, without any income.

Not only that, but Jack also found it was a completely different world that he had to adjust to. He lived with Jenny's sister for the first while. One night while in a pub

---

[13] Apex is used in the travel industry to describe a type of airline fare that is discounted due to certain usage restrictions. These fares tend to be heavily discounted due to numerous restrictions involved and are generally non-refundable.

having his usual drink, things changed. He recalls, "It was in a place called Benoni; the pub was called The Wrecks." As he ordered his usual drink, a conversation struck up between him and another guy at the bar. They chatted about different things, and Jack was soon telling him his story. Jack told him he was a blacksmith to trade, that he had travelled from Scotland in the hope of getting work and that he hoped he would soon bring his young family out to South Africa. Suddenly someone tapped him on the shoulder; a gentleman sitting behind him could not help but overhear the story. He knew of a blacksmith job that was available in his own company! The two men discussed the possibility of employment before Jack took his business card. He was advised to phone on Monday morning, which he did, and soon things began to move quickly. The following day, the company sent a car out to fetch him. He hoped that things were now going to improve.

The boss was a Scots fellow, so perhaps that was why he showed such a keen interest in Jack and received such a warm reception. They seemed very interested in taking him on. However, firstly he was given a theory test which he passed with flying colours. At that point, he could not do anything of a practical nature because he was not insured. After a few days, a temporary permit was organised, and he completed the hands-on part of the test. The company were not disappointed. He was given the job, and his plan began to unfold. After working for the company for several months, he received a phone call from Scotland congratulating him on becoming a father for the second time. The boss overheard him, and after making enquiries, he discovered that Jack had become a dad to his second son, Gerry! He was delighted for him and wanted to know about his Scottish home and family. Jack wondered whether he was suspicious about his home circumstances, but instead, he asked for his wife's phone number. After checking out the story for himself by speaking to Jenny's mother on the phone, he generously arranged and paid for the whole family to come out to South Africa. One Spring morning in early April, Jenny, with two small children, the youngest only eight weeks old, flew out from Scotland to join Jack. The company paid for First Class tickets for the family and gave them a loan to rent a house.

Jenny and the children had to travel to London first. Her dad accompanied her on the journey to the airport, but after he left, Jenny cried until she boarded the plane! Her hands were full: the baby was only weeks old, and Steven was a lively three-year-old. She must have felt very vulnerable. The South African company treated them exceptionally well, paying the whole family to travel in luxury at their expense. However, Jenny insisted on purchasing return tickets rather than an Apex for them all! She wanted to keep a back door open just in case things didn't work out. Jenny described the luxuries on the plane: there was a cot attached to the wall with a Moses basket and all essentials that she needed for the flight. She had never seen anything like it. Steven played football on the plane with another wee lad whilst Jenny was continually worried that they might make the plane crash! Jack and Jenny were at long last reunited, but she could not help feeling homesick.

If only Jack could have found inner happiness as quickly as he found work. There was unhappiness inside him that he could not escape no matter where he tried to settle down to live. He tried drowning his sorrows by drinking more heavily, but the inner darkness only worsened. Unfortunately, he began to drink so excessively that he did not turn up for work. The company tried to support him by putting him on constant night shift, but as in the Newcastle days, he started drinking at night too. Jenny became increasingly unhappy: she never really settled despite being near her sister. She desperately missed her parents, who had so lovingly and patiently supported her throughout all her years. Even after living in South Africa for several months, she had held on to the return tickets and had hidden them amongst the towels in her linen cupboard. No one was taking them away from her, not even the company who had asked her to hand them in!

After three hard months in South Africa, firstly living with her sister and then moving to their own home, Jenny phoned Mammy to say, "I want to come home." Her Mammy told her firmly that there was nothing to come home for; all their belongings were sold. It was a Tuesday morning, and after speaking to her, she decided to try her Daddy, hoping for more encouragement from him! She was the apple of his eye, and without hesitation, he told her to book her flights and return home. One night in July, after only being in the country for a few months, Jack and Jenny secretly planned to leave. Jack could not continue to keep his job because of his heavy drinking, and there seemed no point in staying. They arranged flights back home without informing the company, abandoning their new house and life. The whole family did another 'moonlight flit' and were back in Scotland by Friday! Jenny's sister drove them to the airport, desperately upset that her sister was not remaining with them, whilst Jenny never shed a tear! The company never got in touch with them, and they returned to live again with Jenny's parents until they got their own house, which finally became their family home for the rest of their years.

7 Family Troubles

After the family came home to Coatbridge, Jack's drinking habits continued to worsen, despite family responsibilities. What started with a drink in the pub after work eventually led to him being barred from eight or nine pubs in the local area. He began to build up a reputation for being a violent man, just like his father, and was known by both the police and the bar managers for his aggression. Jack described himself as having a 'street pedigree'. People would avoid him because he was always in trouble with the police.

Although Jenny loved him, she could not cope with how he was living and refused to have him at home when under the influence of drink or drugs. Their marriage and family life could only be described as unstable. Jack swore to himself that his children would never see the violence he had seen when he was young and vowed he would never bring it into the house. So, when Jack went on a drinking binge, he just would not come home. His habit of drinking in different places worsened; he woke up not caring or knowing where he was in the morning. Eventually, he would come crawling back home after a week, sick. Jenny would say, "You can come home, but don't bring your drink with you!" It was ruining his health and his life. There is an old saying that drinkers use: "One's too many; one hundred's not enough!" It was just the way Jack felt.

One day, when desperate for a drink, he stole some money that Jenny had put aside for a school trip for young Steven, and as a result, Steven never got to attend his trip. Jack hated himself for doing such a miserable thing. He was shocked at himself, basically stealing from his son, and in some ways this action helped to bring him to his senses. By this time he was twenty-eight years old and Jenny twenty-seven. They had just been blessed with their third child, a daughter this time, whom they named Alison. Jack became determined that it was time to give up drinking, but when he attempted to stop, it turned out to be much more of a struggle than he thought it would have been. He could not cope with the withdrawal symptoms: the DT's[14] or shakes. He drank to feel good. It began to dawn on him that he now had a real problem; he was an alcoholic. When he did not drink, he would wake around 3 a.m. with the shakes; the only thing that stopped these symptoms was a drink. The urge was overwhelming, and he would have to go and find alcohol somewhere. At first he would bring it home and hide it in different parts of the house, but then, when his supplies ran out, he would set off in the middle of the night and start knocking on the doors of his friends, who he knew would have stock in their houses. He would knock until they answered, and if they did not, he would shout through the letterbox, even in the middle of the night, until they did! Jack had never intended to be a heavy drinker and never set out to become an alcoholic.

Not only was he having problems with drink, but Jack was now addicted to the strong painkillers prescribed for his back pain. When he drank after taking these strong painkillers he would black out, and when he awoke, he had no recollection of what had happened. Sometimes

---

[14] DT stands for delirium tremens – a severe type of withdrawal from alcohol.

he would wake up at the police station and ask the officers why he was there! The police took delight in winding him up and telling him, "You'll find out when you go to court!"

At home Jack's family was facing difficulties. Gerry, their second child, had been born with a disability to his left hand. He was a determined little character, full of life and mischief. Before he began school, he practised tying his laces for hours as he did not want to be the odd one out! However, he was the only one who could tie his laces, so he was the odd one out! He had beautiful big brown eyes and a huge smile and was always a favourite with the girls.

Gerry found school difficult. Before too long, he was coming home from school with a look on his little face that his parents grew to recognise. It left them with a sinking feeling in the pit of their stomachs when they saw the results of cruel bullying due to Gerry's disability. They knew children were making fun of him and found it heartbreaking to watch. Eventually, Jack and Jenny agreed to take Gerry out of the non-denominational school he attended and put him in a Catholic school.[15] There were fewer incidents at the new school, but it was still enough to hit a raw nerve in his dad's heart. It reminded Jack of his childhood and brought painful memories back to him of the taunts he received at school.

---

[15] Schools in Scotland are segregated into Catholic and Non-denominational schools. This was a result of the influx of large numbers of Irish immigrants in the nineteenth century, which led to Catholic schools being established. This segregation still exists.

Jack, unable to deal directly with the children concerned, approached the fathers of the children in the only way he knew how, with violence. He found out where the fathers of these boys drank and would find himself marching into their clubs and pubs, threatening that if they did not deal with their boys, he would deal with them. He caused so much trouble that the police got involved, and Jack's list of criminal offences grew longer.

One day, Jack was sitting in his living room when thirteen-year-old Gerry came in from school. He was in a terrible state of panic and agitation. Jack and Jenny noticed bruising around his neck and asked what had happened. It turned out that he and his two friends had been having a carry-on coming home from school. One of the lads had thrown a stone at Gerry, which had landed in a man's garden. The man had come out to Gerry, got hold of him around his neck, and then gone into Gerry's pocket for ID, took it out, and made threats against him.

Jenny said with a shudder, "You could see the thumbprint and four fingerprints on either side of Gerry's neck." Jack asked Gerry where this man lived, and he sent a message to him saying, "Tell him he'll find me at the school at 2 pm!" Jack, in his own words, said, "I got suited and booted and had just opened the front door when I heard my surname getting mentioned." Looking along the row of houses where he lived, he saw the man concerned speaking to a neighbour, asking where Gerry stayed. Jack immediately confronted him, and a fight broke out. His wife witnessed the whole incident and was shocked! It was the first time she had seen her husband being so violent; the bully ended up in a terrible state.

She knew Jack could be angry but had never seen him like this; she was appalled. Unknown to them both, this man was a neighbour. He lived around the corner from them, where Jack's sister lived. Jack left him alone for two weeks and then went round to his house and told him he wanted him to apologise to Gerry for what he had done. Later, Jack found out that this man had been driven from another housing scheme for bullying children. Jack's sister wasn't too pleased with her older brother for his behaviour, and neither were some of Jack's other neighbours, but when the same man began to cause trouble again with them and their children, they were quick to phone to see if Jack would help. He declined politely and encouraged them to fight their own battles!

Another time, Gerry arrived home from school with the same hurt and withdrawn expression. By this stage, Gerry was in high school. Jack did not need to hear the details of what had been said or who said it; it was enough that his boy was upset over something he should not have been. If Gerry wanted to tell him the details, then Jack was prepared to listen, but on more than one occasion, Gerry came in and said, "Dad, they're down there now with golf clubs. They are starting to wait on me at the school gate." His parents, furious with rage, drove down in the car to the school. Sure enough, there were the four boys concerned, hanging around the school gates carrying golf clubs. Jack got out and approached the boys to speak casually to them, asking what they were doing with the golf clubs. As expected, they began making rude and nasty comments to Jack before running away. Jack quickly got into the car and began to drive towards them. He was more than tempted to pin one of them up against the school fence and still shuddered to think what would have happened if he had, but instead, at the last minute, he turned the steering wheel the other way and drove off. Again, he visited the clubs and pubs to find the boys' fathers. He warned them there would be trouble if they did not sort their boys out. Jack's reputation went before him, even in clubs he had never visited before, and when he gave a warning, the other party knew it would happen if the situation continued. Jack admitted he often ended up in a fight. The fighting led to the police becoming involved, and on more than one occasion Jack assaulted the police too. Violence was his way out of many circumstances.

This was a painful situation for any parent to handle: let alone someone so troubled as Jack. One day when Jack and Jenny were chatting about how they could help Gerry deal with this problem, Jack remembered that he knew someone from one of the rival gangs who had been born with a similar disability to Gerry. When Gerry came home from school that day, Jack took him around to Mr Donnelly's house. He left Gerry in the car as he went up and knocked on the front door. Jack could see the apprehension on Mr Donnelly's face as he opened the door and saw his old rival standing there! Jack explained the situation, and before too long, the door was swung wide open, and both were invited in and given a warm welcome. Mr Donnelly was a big help, explaining how he had coped with the same difficulties whilst growing up. That was a bit of a turning point for Gerry.

Jack began to think of ways to help Gerry toughen up and learn how to cope with these difficulties on his own. He took him to boxing lessons to help him whilst Steven went along too to encourage Gerry and help protect his brother at school. Gerry began to enjoy these training sessions and was so successful that eventually he was offered professional training.

8 From Drink to Alcoholics Anonymous

Despite these rocky times, Jenny always said that Jack was a different person inside their home from the person that others saw outside. When she learned of the things he got involved in outside the home, she could hardly believe it was the same person. He never brought his troubles and violence into the house and was always careful around the children. People used to say to her, 'How can you put up with him?' but she insisted he was not that kind of person at home. He was a good father, kind and caring towards his own family. He said, "I don't think once in my life I've ever lifted my hands to my laddies or Alison. I shouted at Alison one night, and Jenny tells me to this day that the child wet herself! I was very protective of my weans and our George, my brother, always."

Jack decided he would try to turn his life around by attending Alcoholics Anonymous (AA) meetings for his own sake and his family's. He had struggled with his alcohol problem for many years. The AA meetings helped, even though Jack always said it changed him on the outside but not on the inside. At the AA meetings, there was one lad, Alec, who seemed a bit different from the rest of the unsavoury characters he met. After a few weeks of attending the AA meetings, Alec spoke to him and another lad, Tam, and said that they were ready to visit this place with him called the King's. Jack, not understanding what Alec was talking about, asked for clarification. After a few weeks, Alec arranged for Jack and Tam to go to The Kings Church in Motherwell.

They were unprepared for this and did not understand where they were going, why they were there or what they were in for! They spent the church meeting watching what was happening without taking anything in. Looking back, Jack does not think Alec was that serious either because when an altar call was made, he was prodded in the ribs, and not only was he told to put his hand up, but to tell his pal, Tam, to put his hand up too. He looks back now and realises they were all just there for a laugh. Jack said that after they had raised their hands to indicate they wanted something (Jack was unsure what), he and Tam were ushered down some stairs into a basement. As he looked over his shoulder, Alec, who had remained in his seat, was killing himself laughing! Jack remembers being asked to sit on a wee chair in a room (possibly a Sunday School room for children), and as the people began to pray, they laid their hands on his head and spoke in a funny language. He now understands this to be tongues: references to this can be found in the Bible.[16]

After it was all over, Jack made a quick getaway and waited patiently outside for his pal Tam to come out. As Tam approached him, he asked, "How do you feel?" Jack replied laughingly, "I feel like a drink!" But Jack admits, "I've got to tell the truth. I have a vague memory of these people looking happy. That struck me." These Christians wanted the phone numbers of their new contacts, obviously aware of a need for follow-up, but Tam sidestepped it by saying he was not on the phone whilst Jack just backed off. Looking back, Jack realised he was

---

[16] For further information read Bible References: Acts Chapters 1 & 2. The author would also recommend the following books: *The Baptism in the Spirit and its Effects* by Hugh B Black, and *They Speak with Other Tongues* by John & Elizabeth Sherrill.

frightened but never admitted it. Jack must have been drawn, or perhaps it was the faithful prayers of the people of that church because, despite the high jinks, he returned on two future occasions over the years. Sometimes, sitting at home, he would feel inclined to return to the church and ask Jenny to drive him over. One of these occasions was fifteen years later. Jenny was unfamiliar with the area and could not find her way back to The Kings Church, so she dropped Jack off nearby. The Elim Church was just across the road from The Kings Church, and Jack just slipped in and sat at the back. There was a slideshow that night. No one spoke to him, but he sat quietly and watched it. In the end, he phoned Jenny, and she came and picked him up.

Looking back, he realised that God was working on his life even in those early years, although it would take another twenty years before he truly began to find Christ for himself. He said, on reflection, "I do believe that God was trying to get my attention long before I came to Struthers."[17]

He can remember another night when the minister from the local Church of Scotland in Townhead dropped by. Jack had been praying on his hands and knees in the bathroom for help. Jenny called him to say there was someone at the front door. He came downstairs to see that Alec was at the door, this time with a young Church of Scotland minister, Derek, who came in and spoke to Jack for a while. It was as if from time to time God was trying to wake him to something greater, something far

---

[17] Struthers Memorial Church, Cumbernauld, the church that Jack now attends.

more significant that Jack had never realised before, but as yet he was still in the dark, not understanding what others were attempting to show him.

He found the AA meetings helped to some extent. He began to get his drinking under control even if the inner changes he was searching for had not happened yet. Part of the AA 12-step programme requires each candidate to speak confidentially to someone and disclose things that trouble them from their past. Alec and Jack went on a retreat to the local monastery, although Jack admits they were as often in the pub as the retreat! He told me he could remember waking the monks at about 4:30 am, after having had a good drink and speaking to a 'wee monk'. He remembers thinking his eyes were like dark marbles in the middle of the night! Although Jack did not seem genuine in his behaviour, he did admit to opening up and confessing to the monk things that no one else would ever know. He sadly said that although he went through the steps of the programme, it did not stop the torment of the past. It helped him sort his life out for two years on the outside, but he was still the same on the inside.

He continued to attend AA until, at one of the meetings, he discovered that the man sitting opposite him was the one who had been responsible many years ago for his mother's affair! Jack said it dawned on him slowly. To begin with, it was just a suspicion, and then when Jack discovered it was him, he stormed out of the AA meeting and never returned. He blamed this man for destroying his childhood. Despite this difficulty, Jack attempted to change. His efforts were not in vain, and he found an ability to abstain from alcohol. There was a success in a measure. He insisted on calling himself a 'dry drunk' as he wasn't convinced of real inner change! In other words, although he stopped drinking for two years, the cause of his drinking habit remained. And now, to make matters worse, the guys he met on the AA programme had introduced him to other tablets: Librium, Tramadol, Dihydrocodeine – anything that would give him a bit of a glow. The only thing that changed was that he had put a cork in the bottle and was sober for two years, but unfortunately was now hooked on even more pills! He admitted that AA works for some folks but he needed something more and didn't know what that was. He knew there was an arrogance within him that was very wrong and recognised the same arrogant quality in others at AA. Jack knew where his arrogance came from: it stemmed from being badly treated by his father in earlier years. He can remember deciding that no one would ever talk down to him again; he developed a hardness and an arrogance that would defy fear; the same unresolved emotional issues remained from childhood. If someone had crossed him, he would still have taken them outside and fought with them just the same.

On the outside, however, things looked better; Jack remained sober for several years. He even got himself another job and started working as a bricklayer. Everything seemed to be better as long as he stayed away from alcohol. Jenny's family slowly began to accept Jack after struggling with him for years. They started to recognise the genuine person, and he found warmth and acceptance among them. He could still get himself in bother with the police for fighting, but the in-laws were tolerant of Jack as long as there was a smile on their daughter's face.

Sadly, Jenny's dad never lived long enough to see the spiritual transformation in him, but despite that, when he was dying, Jack would go up and sit with him all night. He had a kind heart underneath all the hardness and supported the family through some difficult times.

9 The Drug World

Jack continued using a variety of pills he had been introduced to at AA. They seemed to quell the anger within him, helping him to sleep, and as a result, he ended up taking pills for many years. He was still taking the prescribed Diazepam from the doctor too.

One day, he discovered his brother George was drug dealing. Jack confessed to being angry with him. "I admit," he said, "I went over and black-and-blued him from head to toe. I was raging and totally anti-drugs!" The boys' Mammy found out, and she was furious too. She was worried that George would bring shame to the family name! She shouted at George, who came away with some lame excuse about the fact it was only cannabis, and they were going to legalise it soon anyway. When people were after George for money, Jack would defend him and sort out the problem for him, even though Jack was angry with him for getting into the drug game in the first place. Jack still felt protective and would not let anyone swindle his brother.

One night, George invited Jack to Manchester to watch a boxing match. Jack had a particular love for boxing, so the two brothers booked their tickets and a night in a hotel and set off together. George was at the wheel. Jack had no idea what would be entailed in this journey south!

After a good journey, they arrived and checked in at their hotel in Liverpool. They went to a local restaurant for something to eat before driving to Old Trafford in Manchester, where the fight was being held. It all seemed a pleasant trip to Jack. He had put his money on his favourite boxer, Chris Eubank, and was looking forward to the fight. When they arrived, the place was 'hoaching';[18] crowds jostled as they queued impatiently, waiting to enter and then find their seats. They had a great night, and Jack enjoyed himself immensely, even though the outcome was a draw.

After it was over, George met up with some people he knew and arranged for them to go on to a party. Jack was impressed as the cars drew up to collect their passengers outside the front doors. He had never seen such a fleet of expensive vehicles arriving with young lads at the wheel. It was a short journey to where the party was being held, and celebrations soon got underway. Jack could tell by the way the men were talking that something was afoot. They seemed to be celebrating that one of their own was off to jail on Monday! Jack felt wary and decided to try and keep his distance. He wandered through the house until he found a quieter room, saying he would try to catch up on some sleep. When it came time for the two brothers to leave, an arrangement was made for them to stop off somewhere on their way back to Liverpool. Jack followed his brother to the car. He tried to overhear the details of where they were going but could not make it out. The two brothers drove several miles before George finally drew up outside a huge mansion. It was dark outside, but Jack could make out gardens protected by a high fence and electric gates. As the gates opened, George drove into the long drive and parked near the house's front entrance. They waited a few minutes until some men came out to meet them. George opened the door as the

---

[18] Full of or swarming with people or things

strangers approached. They stood at the back of the car, talking in low voices. Jack, sitting in the passenger seat, listened to the quiet voices and watched what was happening in the wing mirror. He could see in the tail lights one of the men giving George a spare tyre. This was Jack's first inkling that something dodgy was going on. He clocked it straight away and was out of the car like a shot. He turned to the stranger and said, "No, no, mate, I'm not getting involved ... " But his brother had other plans and pacified Jack, saying it would be okay. Before long, the spare tyre was in the boot of their car, and the two brothers had set off for their hotel again. For the first time, he began to realise the size of the drug operation his brother was involved in. He wanted no part whatsoever in any of it!

He did not realise that these guys were assessing him at the same time as they were working with George. He only fully understood this when three years later, two of these guys looking for a favour turned up at his house one night in Coatbridge. As Jack explained in his own words, they were looking to see if he had the 'pedigree' - the ability to cope in dangerous situations. If you were going to deal with drugs, you had to know how to deal with any problem without panicking and running to the police.

It all happened like this: Jack had just celebrated his fortieth birthday. He was sitting in his living room watching the television one night with Jenny when they heard a knock at the front door. They were not expecting anyone, so he was surprised to see two men he had seen at the large house in Liverpool standing on his doorstep, asking him for a favour. They were holding a parcel and asked him if he would hold on to it for a few days for them, offering to pay him a large sum of money. One of their contacts had fallen through, so they had thought he would be able to help. Without warning, they turned up at his house, looking for a favour. The young couple had little money for their growing family, and Jack couldn't resist the offer. It seemed harmless enough at the time. He still was not getting involved in anything wrong. He was looking after a parcel for someone, so he accepted it, asked no questions, and was duly paid £500-600 in cash. And that was the start, the green light for the dealers to use Jack. A small favour that ended up almost ruining his whole life. There was a 'dry-up' in cannabis in Scotland at the time. In other words, very little cannabis was being produced in Scotland. Drugs were brought from Ireland via Liverpool and Manchester into the country and transported to Scotland to meet the demand. These guys continued to work with George, and now they had roped Jack into their operation.

"Getting into drugs came by accident," Jack admitted. "You don't go into it knowing you are going to destroy lives or that you're going to meet unsavoury people or become one of them yourself. It all just patterns out." Jenny spoke later of the temptation of that moment and all that followed. She said, "We didn't have a bean. We couldn't even afford to buy the kids treats, and suddenly there was this cash in hand, and instantly, we could treat the children, take them to the cinema and all the other things we wanted to do." Little did they know, this small wrong choice would only lead to much worse.

Jack soon began to work with these men regularly. The whole thing quickly spiralled into a big drug operation and a different way of life for him. He was holding drugs for these men and began to travel south three or four times a week to Liverpool to collect the goods. An elderly gentleman, Frank, who was the head man in the whole operation, lived in the large house that Jack had visited earlier with his brother. He said it worked like this: he would arrive at the said gentleman's home, who would ask what kind of car he had, and then a spare tyre would be produced for that particular make of car. Everything would be carefully weighed out and then stored within the spare wheel, which would be hurriedly removed from the house and placed in the boot of his car. Then Jack would be invited back into the house for a drink. Frank would never touch any of the drugs he was selling and never took drugs. A clever, cruel dealer who had been involved in the drug world for a long time and benefitted enormously from the trade!

Before long, Jack's drug business grew and with it came greater responsibilities. He was given keys to six or seven houses within a mile of his family home in Coatbridge. These were the drug dens. He was working for the men who owned these houses. Jack had never acquired a driving licence; he had only ever had a couple of driving lessons, although he had been driving a BMW for years. Jack had obtained a false driving licence and documents, just in case he was ever stopped by the police.

Even though the first point of contact had been George, now Jack got heavily involved in the drug scene. He would drive south to collect his drugs, his only contact being a phone number. He phoned from a phone box or café, received details of the pick-up and then would eat or chew the number before proceeding to his destination, often a big farmhouse out in the country. These guys were picking up a kilo for £2,000. Before too long, Jack was coming up the road with five kilos of cannabis.

Once it was in his possession, he was responsible for hiding it, selling it, and making money. He could make £4,000 in a night, five nights a week! It did not take long for people to know he had drugs to sell. Although he continued to make more money than he had ever dreamt of, he discovered that with drugs came trouble. Before too long it came to his home, and Jack had no option but to deal with it. His phone would go continually. He said he could remember his father-in-law being around at the house one Christmas. Jack had told his contacts not to get in touch at Christmas, but there were no mobiles these days, so the house phone rang all night. Jack said it was like a hotline! His father-in-law never asked a question or said a word about it, although Jack reckoned he knew what was happening. Through this, he got to know people from all parts of the local area and built up his reputation and drug business.

10 The Beginning of the End

It seemed only natural that Jack would eventually begin to experiment with drugs, and this was the beginning of the end of his success as a dealer. He tried cannabis but found he didn't like it. Cannabis, he explained to me, is meant to relax a person, but it left him with his guard down, feeling on overdrive and vulnerable. There was too much damage inside for Jack to cope with relaxing! Before long, he had moved on to dealing and experimenting with Ecstasy: he loved the glow it gave him. He would buy ten bags in one night. Each bag would contain a thousand pills, giving Jack ten thousand in his keeping. Stashing them in one of his houses, Jack would double the price to sell to the street dealer. He was soon making a considerable amount of money. Yet this wasn't enough. Before long, he moved on to taking and dealing cocaine. He said the first time he took a little bit of cocaine made him feel on top of the world, like a football celebrity, after only a couple of lines! However, this feeling didn't last long until it slowly began to drag him down into a steady decline. Nothing seemed to satisfy him, because he then moved on to crack cocaine and even experimented with heroin. All through this time, he never touched alcohol. Jack was smart enough to know he needed his wits about him!

Unfortunately, as Jack began to build up a reputation with the street dealers, he also began to build up a reputation with the police. The drug squad heard the careless whispers. They came down heavily on anyone who was dealing hard drugs. Again and again the police would warn Jack and let him know they were watching him by busting his house and breaking down his front door. In fact, on one of these occasions, he was arrested and remanded in custody. Thankfully for Jack, the case collapsed. Eventually, he got to the stage where he didn't care so much about the money: it was all about cops and robbers, the buzz and the chase, and he liked that!

But life was fast-moving for Jack, and it wasn't long before things became even more dangerous for him. Jack's phone would be continually ringing with people looking for drugs whilst he was in one of his drug dens. Friday nights were the busiest! He would be sorting this one and that one out, making sure they had their supplies, and then another would phone, and he would arrange to meet them somewhere locally. He said they had names for different places. One of his meeting places was at the back of the church, nicknamed the graveyard, although there was no graveyard there!

Jack eventually found himself in far too many menacing situations for his liking. He found he constantly had to change his routine, continually moving from drug den to drug den, because if he created a regular pattern when dealing, the drug squad would soon recognise his movements. One day, he was in one of his dens, dealing, when someone he was friendly with came into the room. The lad was agitated and said to Jack, "There are three guys in there who have just come in (pointing to the other room), and they're getting a bit rowdy!" Jack went through to the other room to find out who they were. He discovered it was guys he didn't know. He demanded to know their names and why they were there. He only allowed people in his houses he knew, and he certainly wouldn't have dealt drugs to strangers. The three men told Jack their names, and when Jack realised he did not know where these guys had come from, he and his pal chucked them out of the house. Jack thought no more about it. The next day, he and his pal decided to go to another of his dens to take cocaine together. After several hours, they were startled as the door came flying off its hinges! Suddenly, Jack was surrounded by men from the CID. They demanded to know where Jack had been the night before, paying no attention to the drugs and pipes lying around the floor. Jack had no idea what was going on! He later learned that the three guys he had kicked out of the house the day before had returned that night with hammers and a machete looking for him. They found someone and mistook him for Jack, and almost killed him. At that particular moment, as the CID was cross-examining Jack, the unfortunate fellow was in a hospital on a ventilator. The police thought Jack had been involved. Thankfully his pal had been with him the whole time and could vouch for him.

There is often a world within worlds that the majority of people know very little about. Jack, by this time, was no stranger to the underworld. He soon made some phone calls to his contacts to come and deal with these guys who were after him. It wasn't that he couldn't deal with them, but he had to keep clear now that the police were on the lookout. And so that's exactly what happened.

Jack was lucky this time, but there were many times when he was caught red-handed. He said if he got caught, he would admit he had committed the crime, although he was always advised to make the usual 'no comment' at the interview by his lawyer. Before his life was eventually turned around, he had three sheriff and jury trials at the High Court and walked out of all three because witnesses never turned up! He did not want to go into gory details, and I respected him for that, but as he explained, "It gives you an idea of the life I was living."

He told me a little about one of these incidents. One night two men from the CID came to his house and asked where he was on a particular night. Jack had been involved in a robbery that night, but he thought he had got away with it because although the police had questioned him at the time, he had not heard anything more from them. However, eight months had passed, and they returned to interrogate him further. Once more, they busted his house. They took Jack upstairs, kept Jenny downstairs, and said they were arresting him for armed robbery. Jack was confused. He did not understand that this was related to the incident eight months ago, but before he had time to figure out what was happening, he was handcuffed and taken to the police station. The CID announced, "You can say what you want and do what you like, but your DNA is all over the place!" Jack suddenly realised which incident they were talking about; his blood had been left at the scene! That particular case was a solemn case to be tried before a sheriff and jury, but the trial collapsed because again no witnesses turned up. The truth is, he had been involved in an armed robbery, but when he realised the person they were robbing was elderly he refused to take part in it, and so the guys involved in the operation who were with him turned on him! Although Jack managed to get away, his blood by this point was all over the crime scene.

He believed in standing his ground when working out on the streets. Perhaps it was this belief that made him successful as a dealer in his early days. He asserted that if you thought you were right in a situation, you could deal confidently with others, knowing that you would never lose. He said, "If you're right, you can stand up and be counted, but if you're wrong, you grow nervous and find yourself tongue-tied." He recognised that this train of thought helped him through the next set of problems which confronted him. Jack will never forget the night two guys came to visit him in his house and threatened him as they placed guns on his coffee table in the living room.

One day Jack was in one of his local dens dealing drugs to some guys. He was also using drugs himself at the time. George, his brother, and Gerry, Jack's second son, had been telling him they had heard that Gerry's girlfriend's dad had a bar of cannabis hidden in his house. A bar of cannabis was 9oz, and its value was near £8,000. Jack did not believe Gerry and responded, "nobody keeps a bar of cannabis in their house!" Gerry made a joke that he would find out and steal it if it was there.

Jack did not remember any more than this. He reckons, looking back, that he fell asleep, probably under the influence of cocaine, and the next thing he knew was he could hear Jenny's voice urgently waking him up. He looked up to find eight or nine guys around him. As he roused himself from his drug stupor and tried to fathom what was going on, he discovered that George and Gerry had done it! They had gone and stolen the 9oz bar of cannabis! Now it became Jack's problem to sort out. He knew he would need to pay the money back to someone if he was going to protect George and Gerry.

These things take time to sort out. Within a short time, Jack found and returned a certain amount of the stolen drug package and offered to pay for the rest with cash. One afternoon, a month later, when Jack was in his home, four guys came to collect the money. He had been expecting a visit at any time from the men concerned. After all, it was his son who had taken the drugs! He did not want any more trouble. When these men arrived at his home, he had a hidden tape recorder set up to record the whole conversation which was to take place. Sure enough, Jack paid them £3,500–£4,000 and recorded the conversation on tape. To his great relief, all went well. Everybody appeared friendly by the time the men left his house. His son was safe, and he assumed that was the end.

However, about a year later, one Saturday afternoon, Jack and Jenny had gone out for the day to Strathclyde Park. Jenny was playing mini bingo whilst Jack was in the pub having a few beers and watching a football match on the TV. His phone rang, and someone at the end of the phone asked to speak to him. Jack sensed immediately that something was not right. He did not recognise the voice. He felt on his guard during the conversation that followed and did not ask any questions or ask how they had managed to get hold of his number. The stranger at the end of the phone said in a threatening voice, "You owe us money! We'll be coming over to see you." Jenny arrived shortly after that, and he began telling her about the call when his phone rang again. This time, it was his sister Carol. She sounded scared. She said, "Jack, there are two guys in my house, and they are asking me lots of questions. Jack, I'm terrified!" He thought it must have been one of the men who had phoned him earlier. He realised that he was dealing with a couple of nasties when they were threatening his family. Jack asked to speak to them, and again the threat was repeated to him that he would be getting a visit from them. He felt incredibly uptight about the situation but could only wait to find out what it was all about. They had not given him any names, but he knew they would appear at his home soon and would be looking for money.

Jack will never forget the Sunday afternoon they arranged to come to his house. He was at home with his pal, wee Sammy, and was telling him he was expecting a bit of trouble. He had already arranged for Jenny to leave the house as he did not want her to be in a dangerous situation. The doorbell rang, and Jack could see through the glass door two men standing outside, waiting. He turned to Sammy and explained that these two wanted to see him alone and that there might be some problems. Immediately Sammy became defensive and was ready for a fight, but Jack, wanting to avoid trouble, told him he had to leave. He opened the front door a fraction and said, "Round the back!" The guys came to his back door, and Jack let them in whilst Sammy went out the front door.

The first man came in and sat on the couch. He said, "We're carrying," as he put his gun down on Jack's table. The second man glared threateningly at Jack, indicating he was carrying a gun too. They were trying to intimidate him. Jack looked confused and asked, "Whit's this all about?" The two men said he owed them money because he had taken a bar of cannabis.

Jack now understood the situation; they were referring to the cannabis that Gerry, his son, had stolen some time ago. He stood his ground, telling them the money was already paid back. He soon got the tape recorder out, put batteries in it and let them hear the conversation that he had recorded sometime before. The guys who were after money were not satisfied with this. They were looking for ready cash. They told Jack they wanted to speak to Gerry and did not move. Jack was as obstinate as they were and turned to them and said, "Well, I am not bringing him up today. You can speak to him another day." Jack refused to bring Gerry into a situation without rehearsing what he would say! Again, the men pressurised him to get Gerry immediately, but Jack remained firm. He asked them what kind of money they were talking about, and the guys said £4–5,000. Eventually, they left, much to Jack's relief, saying they would return in a couple of days.

As soon as they left, Jack phoned Gerry. The two got together to rehearse their story and what they would say to the men. Jack decided to call their bluff and told Gerry to tell them he still owed £300. He thought if the men got something out of this, they would leave them alone. A few days later, it was arranged for these men to come back to the house. They arrived before Gerry and sat in Jack's living room, waiting for the lad to appear. When Gerry arrived, they watched as the terrified youngster slunk into his own dad's house. They were trying to suss him out, but all they could see was a scared young lad! After asking him several questions, Gerry gave them the rehearsed answers he and Jack had practised, explaining he still owed £300. They demanded cash from him. Jack was all organised and had already stashed the money away. He handed the two guys the £300, and they all shook hands amicably and left.

Jack knew they were a couple of troublemakers just out of jail looking for an easy way to get hold of some cash. He reckoned they had heard that he had paid the money back for the stolen cannabis bar and thought it would be easy to pressurise him for more money. Jack would not fold, not even when the threat of guns came into his home.

Later, he learned that after these two men had left, they went and burned down the flat of a guy who was hassling them for money! Jack refused to feel threatened by these two men. Being the kind of person he was, he kept in touch with them and, before too long, began working with them. They would sell drugs to him in bulk as they were more experienced players than he was, and he would sell them to others in the street. Jack explained that he continued to work with others in the drug game. He told me that if you show a sign of weakness, people will walk right over the top of you. Your word is your honour; a handshake is a mutual agreement. He acknowledged that it is a different world out there.

He continued making money for the next two or three years before his drug habit finally got the better of him and began to affect his health badly. He could not cope with the responsibilities, and soon the door closed, the money ran out, and the friends disappeared. He was still attempting to deal drugs, although not on the scale he had been before. Jack was in the position where someone in the street would give him several kilos of hash. He was no longer the first point of contact in the drug circle and was now being charged for the drugs he was buying. He was buying them and selling them to others. Jack called it a 'lay-on' when someone gave you a certain number of drugs. He was responsible for the money being collected and returned to the dealer. Even if the drugs were confiscated by the drug squad or not sold, he would be held accountable. By now his addiction had a grip on him. He was buying cocaine for his personal use with any money he was making from selling hash, and so, when the dealers, higher in the drug chain, were coming to collect their debt, Jack did not have it because he had already spent it. His drug habit became critical, he was no longer in any fit state to deal drugs, and eventually, he hit an all-time low with his addiction. He was smoking crack cocaine and then snorting it. He gradually lost control not only of his drug deals but of himself too. After five or six years of this kind of lifestyle, things were taking their toll, and he found he was grasping at straws, frantically trying to cope with life as he knew it. He reckoned he must personally have used £120–130,000 worth of drugs. The effects of cocaine were horrendous, and Jack found he had to use at least three grams to stop the shakes. It wasn't long before he ended up in the hospital, overdosing. He admits, "I'm a lucky man. I should be dead!"

He knew it was the end of the road for him. His luck had run out, and he began to cut down the amount of cocaine he was taking, partly because he had no choice. He was past the point of begging on the street for money. Jack said, "I'll be honest with you, I had too much pride in me to go and beg. I had done that, walking about the streets begging for money." So, he began to suffer as he went through the withdrawals. He said his whole body ached, but the inner darkness he faced was far worse. His withdrawals from drugs took him into a spiral of depression. As he began to face reality, the wrong choices he had made, and the lives he had affected, made him feel suicidal; he was in a murky hole of despair. He became desperate for anything to help him. He needed something to block out the depression and darkness he felt round about his soul. Once again, Jack began to drink heavily.

It all happened so quickly. It was as if Jack just threw himself right back into his old drinking habits. He tried to hide much of his unhappiness during this time. He knew if he started to drink, he would not stop, so when the urge came over him, he would leave home. After being out of the house for several days at a time on a drinking binge, he would arrive home, put on a false face, and pretend everything was rosy in the garden. But there were times when Jack would go on a drinking binge and not come back. Jenny would grow worried. When he disappeared for long periods, Steven, their eldest son, now in his early twenties, would go on a dad hunt! He would eventually find out where his dad was, often in one of his drug dens, and come back and tell Jenny. Together they would drive down to fetch him and bring him home. Steven would hoist his dad over his shoulder, and between the two of them, they would struggle to get him downstairs and into the car. Jenny said, "The alcohol was so strong smelling they had to wind down the windows in the car to cope!"

There were times after these occasions when his withdrawals were so awful that Jenny would have to go and buy him cans of lager and bring them home. She would give him one can to settle him to get rid of the shakes and another several hours later. That seemed to work until Jack gave in and went on another drinking spree. That is just the way he was.

Jack knew things would have to change. Eventually, he began the long battle to break his addictions and face the withdrawal symptoms from alcohol and drugs, which he was still taking from time to time. He described the terrible fear, anxiety and lack of confidence that would come over him as he began this process. At times Jack would try to make his way down to the corner shop five minutes from home. On the way, he could not speak to anybody because he was so anxious. He would purchase four cans of lager and then go into the phone box and drink two cans, after which he managed to return home without the shakes. After two cans, he found he could cope again. He explained, "You feel petrified. Your whole body is shaking. I would go into the corner shop without money, and they sometimes put it on a tab for me. There were times when I couldn't get any cans, and then in desperation, I would jump on the counter to shoplift. I would get lifted by the police for robbery. After being taken to court several times, I got barred from the shops. It was a dark place." Again, Jack was arrested and held in Barlinnie Prison for a short time. The case collapsed again, and he was soon released. He knew by this point that he was reaching an all-time low.

He tried not to let Jenny know his inner thoughts. He found himself in a dark, dark place. As he began to sober up, he started to face the consequences of his actions. He felt embarrassed by his behaviour as a man. What kind of human being was he? What kind of husband and father? He spoke of the terrible depression that engulfed him: feelings of being a total failure and utterly worthless to his family. Emotions were surfacing with which Jack could scarcely cope. He began to face how far he had fallen from the start of his drinking and drug career. On occasion, he lost the will to live and tried numerous times to take his life. Again and again he was spared. He does not know how many hospitals he has been in after trying to take his life. He said, "It wasn't a cry for help. I just wanted out of this life, selfishly, I may add. When you mix booze, drugs, and anger, that's a bad combination. That's when you get into trouble with the police. You're lying in a muckhole. Alison Speirs[19] describes it as lying in slime. You think you're never going to get out."

There was one occasion when Jack had given in and was on a bender.[20] He had gone to bed drunk. Steven had gone upstairs to check if Jack was okay. The next moment, Jenny heard Steven shouting in alarm. As she rushed upstairs to find out what was wrong, she found Jack unconscious on the floor and saw that one side of his face was distorted. They thought it was a stroke and phoned an ambulance immediately. By the time they got Jack to the hospital, he had come round, and there was no evidence of a stroke despite the horrible fright it had given them.

---

[19] Alison Speirs is the minister of our Glasgow branch of Struthers Memorial Church. Her testimony can be found in the book *Revival: Personal Encounters* by H B Black. Although Alison didn't suffer from addiction in the way Jack had, her sense of conviction of sin was nevertheless as profound, and her conversion experience as remarkable. The author, Mr Hugh Black, was one of the founders of the group of churches known as Struthers Memorial Church.

[20] Bender – slang term for heavy drinking session.

Jenny explained that things became so intolerable at home, with the heavy drinking sessions and the depression, that at one point she left Jack and went to stay with Gerry for three months. She couldn't cope any longer. She was working as a carer and, despite her worries, had to be very strong and carry on regardless, going to work. As she went to and from work, she would pass her home and notice the blinds were never opened, and she grew worried. It was a dark time for them both. She would phone Jack and encourage him to get up, get washed and dressed and go out for lunch together, but she always refused to go back home to him. She was determined to make him stop drinking. After their lunch date, she would drop him at the door and return to her son's house again.

Jack eventually asked the doctor for help and was put on Antabuse medication. He soon discovered he became violently ill when he drank on these occasions! This at least discouraged him for the time being.

However, it was a constant battle to make the right choices to break the addiction. Jenny eventually came home when things seemed a bit better, although if someone phoned Jack to go out for a drink, he would occasionally give in and go out. These occasions could still turn into a two-or three-day bender, but Jenny noticed he seemed quieter within himself when he returned home, and she felt things were beginning to calm down. Eventually, Jack seemed more settled and would stay home with her rather than go out. Despite his depression, he tried to help her and would do as much as he could around the home. She would come in from work to an immaculately clean house. She knew Jack was trying but said it was a sad time seeing her husband so low, having lost so much. Thankfully, things were going to take a turn for the better before too long.

86

11 Transformation

It was in 2010 that Jack first came along to the church. By this time, he had a long list of offences that began in his early teens: driving illegally, not paying for his TV licence, shoplifting, violence, robbery and assault, to name some of them. In his bad old days, he got so used to being lifted by the police that when he went to court, he took a bag with him which was already packed. This made things more convenient for his family; he accepted that he would probably end up in jail. On arrival at his new accommodation at the jail, the prison officer was puzzled about how he had acquired all his belongings so quickly. Jack told him cheerfully, "I just brought them with me!"

He told a story about one time being taken to court. He assumed he was being taken to the 'monkey court', the nickname for the court in Coatbridge, but for whatever reason, he was taken to the Cumbernauld Court on this particular occasion. When Jack was released, he asked the police officers for a lift home, but they refused, telling him he would need to walk. Jack wasn't prepared to walk that far – it was a distance of over eight miles! He didn't have any money and so, in the end, went round all the bus drivers in the bus station and begged 50p from each of them. Eventually, he had enough bus fare to get home with £1.50 left over, which he spent on four cans of lager at the local corner shop!

On another occasion when he was at court his mum became seriously ill, and he heard that she was dying. A solicitor came down to see him and told him he was getting a commitment for trial. He also explained to Jack that his mum had taken a turn for the worse and was not expected to pull through. Jack became desperate to be with her at the end of her days. He knew he was in deep trouble. In court that day two men were testifying against him. However, during the trial the witnesses' stories didn't add up, so Jack was released on bail. He was very relieved as now he could spend time with his mum at the end of her life.

Life was now beginning to calm down considerably for Jack compared to his earlier wild days, although he was still binge drinking from time to time. Deep down, Jack knew nothing had changed inside him from his early twenties when he drank heavily to now when he was drinking heavily in his fifties. He would go back to the usual houses to be with the drinkers who were just like himself and would wake up in the morning on someone's couch in the same familiar dark place. He occasionally indulged in the odd night of taking drugs, but no more than this. Jack was getting older, perhaps beginning to slow down a bit, which led to him leading a slightly more stable lifestyle, but by this point his son Gerry was in a terrible way with drink and drugs, and both parents were deeply concerned for him.

It says in the Bible that "All things work together for good",[21] and so it was that God used Gerry's habit to bring Jack and Jenny back to church again, and this time to our church[22]. Jenny worked alongside a Christian lady called Margaret (known as 'Mags'). The two became friends: Mags had shared something of her faith in Christ,

---

[21] Romans 8:28.KJB

[22] Struthers Memorial Church, Cumbernauld.

and in return, Jenny found herself sharing a little of Gerry's troubles. Mags, who has an outstanding testimony to the changing power of Christ,[23] told Jenny all about the Teen Challenge bus[24] that was coming to Coatbridge and all about her church, hoping that one of these might help them. Jenny and Jack decided to bring Gerry to church, although Jack admitted he was a nonbeliever. In desperate moments he had been on his knees in a police station praying, "Get me out of this one!" but this was the first time he had come to church for help. However, even now, he was seeking help for Gerry, not himself. He regarded himself as an atheist and did not believe in any religion but hoped that something might help his son.

What Jack did not understand then, however, was that over the years God the Holy Spirit was drawing him despite himself. There had been those earlier occasions when he had gone to The King's Church and then had felt drawn to return on at least two separate occasions to the same place, and the time he had sought out help at the monastery in the middle of the night, and his prayers of desperation in jail. Something had been happening in Jack's spirit for a long time, but he didn't understand what it was or who was stirring his soul.

Jack's memories of his first church service with us are vague. That evening, a young man called Gavin shared

---

[23] Mags's testimony can be found on our Instagram account (@struthers_cumbernauld).

[24] Teen Challenge – a registered charity that operates nationally to help young people who have developed life-controlling problems, especially drug and alcohol addictions. They use a bus to reach out to the community.

his testimony. He came from a life of drink and drugs to Christ. This made an impression on the family and, in particular, on Jack. Jack knew nothing about Christianity and couldn't explain what a Christian was, but he identified with Gavin and recognised some of the same troubles he'd had. He saw a glow around him when he was speaking.

As minister of the church and in charge of the service that night, I was aware of this new family amongst us. They seemed likeable, but I could see that the son was in great need. He was sitting between his parents and seemed slightly nervous or agitated. Often when visitors come, I find the most effective way of reaching them is to have a testimony from someone they may relate to. I am experienced enough to know that the sermon is not the only thing to impact most folks when they first attend church!

At the end of the service, a lady called Carol spoke to the family and made them welcome. She was friendly and outgoing, and Jack suddenly opened up to her, telling her things he had no intention of talking about. Before too long, Carol asked Jack if he would like to go for prayer, and after he agreed, he found himself in the vestry with me.

Recently when we were chatting about these events, Jack wanted me to know that he was not under any influence that night and was as sober as he is now. He was still taking tablets that he should not have been, but at the time of coming to church and coming for prayer, he was straight and clear-headed.

Some of the details of my first meeting with Jack are vague now, as it was a long time ago. However, neither of us will ever forget the impact of the power of God we felt as we prayed together. Jack came into the vestry asking for help and told me he did not know how to pray. He must have indicated that he wanted to be a Christian, because I remember leading him through the sinner's prayer,[25] and I wouldn't have done that unless he had asked me for that kind of help. At the end of the prayer, I encouraged him to relax, breathe in and say the name of Jesus. What happened next, I will never forget. As Jack began to relax and breathe in, the power of God fell on him, and he began to tremble violently. I encouraged him to say the name of Jesus out loud, but what came out instead could only be described as a growl which eventually turned into deep cries. We prayed until the deep cries quietened, and peace descended on him. In Jack's own words, he said, "I can remember screaming and shaking uncontrollably, and something was

---

[25] Sinner's prayer – a prayer that can be said at the beginning of the Christian journey by one who seeks to change their way of life; it can be repeated after another. To be truly effective, it must be said genuinely from the heart with a deep desire for change. The author has used this method of leading people to Christ many times over and found it to be very effective. Often the person repeating the prayer has described a lightness as the feeling of guilt and sin lifts and, in its place, there comes a sense of cleansing and forgiveness. There have been some remarkable results after such a prayer. On one occasion, an alcoholic went home and poured a bottle of whisky down the sink and never touched another drop of alcohol again, apart from one occasion when he fell out with his wife! That night, he had a couple of lagers, and suddenly finding he was on shaky ground, came and spent the evening with me in our home. The sinner's prayer is more than just repeating a formula – the words of the prayer can be different each time. It is vitally important to see the action of God touching and changing each individual as they come to Him in prayer.

happening, but I didn't know it was God till after I had finished."

There was no time for any explanations. Jack was on God's 'operating table'; I was simply an observer. It wasn't for me to stop the hand of the Divine Surgeon and begin to explain to this stranger what was happening! The proceedings lasted for less than five minutes before peace came, and Jack uttered a few syllables in an unknown language, which he now knows to be tongues. He was visibly shaken, and I remember asking him if he was okay. He indicated he needed a drink of water, so I ran to the kitchen to get him one. It was a change from my normal sprint to fetch tissues! We sat quietly for a few minutes until Jack said, "What was that?" I began to explain, in the simplest terms, that he had just met God and that this was the beginning of a new life for him. It has been one of the most remarkable salvation experiences I have witnessed.

I was privileged to witness the wonderful miracle of salvation that only the Holy Spirit can bring about when a soul is born again.[26] No one can do this for an individual. No one but God can give a person a brand-new beginning or 'wipe their slate' clean, making a soul feel released from their past. God had been drawing Jack for many years, using different people, churches and circumstances along the way, and I had the privilege of seeing the outcome. Here was the result of the long years of desperation and the inner cry for help.

As Jack left the vestry that night, he was a changed

---

[26] The Gospel of John 3:3–7 explains this.

man. He described his feelings in his own words: "After leaving you in the room, as I walked out the double doors, it was as if someone had taken a bit of banding wire and removed the stress. I was tensed up all the time. Something changed in me that night. I stopped drinking, and the swearing disappeared. That night I knew something had happened to me there with no doubting it."

Jack stopped drinking. Knowing the whole story makes me realise the miracle that took place on that occasion. Jack knew he had had an encounter with God in the vestry. Later he told me he didn't even know if I had laid hands on him. Jack was convinced he was not the kind of person who could be easily influenced, but he knew something had happened that night. He had experienced a power, but the understanding of it was not there yet; he was not ready for all that.

Meanwhile, as Jack was receiving prayer, poor Jenny stood waiting in the church, chatting with Carol. She was taken by surprise when she heard someone screaming in the vestry. She felt afraid and said to herself, "What's going on in there?". She turned and asked Carol, standing with her, what the noise was. Carol said, "That's your man!" She was wearing a big smile and looked very happy! Poor Jenny couldn't understand it and all of a sudden felt very wary. They all seemed such decent people, and she had enjoyed the singing, but she couldn't understand this, and to be honest, she did not like it. On the return journey home, he refused to drive illegally, so she had to drive the car! When they got home, she could not believe the change in him. There was no more swearing, and what seemed bizarre was that when he did slip up, he asked God's forgiveness! She was puzzled why she did not find what Jack found; that seemed strange too since she was the one who knew more about the church, having attended Sunday School as a child. However, despite all these confusing things, she could not help noticing that Jack was calm and the tension in the house had gone.

After a few weeks of attending church, not only did Jenny come for prayer and give her life to Christ, but to their joy, Gerry came too. Again, the change was remarkable: he stopped taking drugs, and he stopped drinking. God had wrought a miracle in his heart. His partner, Nicole, thought she was going out with a different guy and said it was brilliant! Jenny said, "I thought I'd died and gone to heaven. There was no drink, there were no drugs, and there was now a different way of life. We have often sat together wondering what would have happened if we hadn't found a church and found God – where would our lives have been?"

When he first started attending the church, Jack was on a daily dose of 30mg of Diazepam for back pain. This was a strong dosage. Jack slowly realised that something was wrong when he took these drugs. His conscience had become sensitive to an inner voice, and he knew he had to listen carefully, so he spoke to his doctor and asked him to reduce it. The doctor started reducing the dosage that Jack was on, and Jack was soon down to 10mg and then an even smaller dose. He believed God helped him, making it easier for him to come off the prescribed drugs, despite the terrible side effects of shaking and sleepless nights.

On an occasion when he had shared his testimony at church, one of the doctors in the congregation came over and asked Jack if he was still on 30mg of Diazepam a day.[27] She was shocked that he had been prescribed this for so long! Not only had he been on these, but he had been taking a variety of tablets bought on the street at the time: Dihydrocodeine and Co-codamol, to name only two.

One of the earliest changes he noticed was when someone swore or blasphemed in his company. He felt slightly shocked despite previously having done the same all his days! No one said anything to him about these things being wrong. He just knew within himself. This is the witness of the Holy Spirit, who convicts us of sin and righteousness.[28]

He found it took longer to give up smoking.[29] Jack had

---

[27] We are not critical of the work our doctors do every day, but sometimes a person needs to reassess their situation with the support of their doctor. We never, as a general rule, encourage people to stop taking medicine that has been prescribed to them unless they feel that they have no more need for it.

[28] Gospel of John 16:8.

[29] We have noticed a pattern when people come from backgrounds where addiction has been prevalent. Smoking is often one of the last addictions to go and requires a strong will, much prayer and discipline. We believe that God can deliver in a moment if He chooses, but often the new convert learns many valuable lessons during this time of conflict when God seems to withhold His power to overcome. I have been asked, 'Why did God not set me free from smoking the way He set me free from drink or heroin?' The answer is, 'I don't know,' but I do know that once victory has been obtained in this area, the new convert will often reflect on how much they learned about themselves and how God deals with a soul during these

smoked since his early teens, the best part of fifty years, but after years of perseverance, he also found victory in this area.

Some months later, we were visiting Jenny and Jack in their home when the police arrived at the door. Jack went outside to speak to them and said, "You'll get no more bother out of me because I've become a Christian." He said, "Just look into my eyes and see the difference. I'm telling the truth; I wouldn't lie to you." Jack thought the policeman recognised his straight-talking and understood there had been a change.

They began to attend church on Saturday night, Sunday morning and Sunday night. Jack said, "It's all right going to church, but you've got to follow the gospel, listen to it, and absorb it." As Jack continued to go to church, he knew it was all about God, but he found it difficult to believe some of the teachings in the gospels. He said, "It was all there in front of me in the Gospel of John, but I just couldn't grasp it." This was to follow later.

---

times. This can be valuable later in their Christian walk, to learn about the dealings of God with the soul.

12 Trials and Failures

Jack and Jenny had been attending church regularly for about two years when they had their first head-on collision with the powers of darkness. It came, as it would come to many parents, through troubles their children faced. On this occasion, it was Gerry.

Jack felt he was beginning to understand the basics of the Christian faith when the storm arose. Their son Gerry, who had unfortunately backslidden and returned to some of his former troubles, was attacked. He was stabbed in the head, and despite the offer of help and support that the family was given from the church, they felt they were not strong enough to handle this one. Jack returned to his old ways of taking control and sorting the situation.

It is worth saying at this point that he did not have any intention of leaving the church, but circumstances overtook him, and within a short time, he returned to his old way of life. He struggled to do the right thing to begin with, but he discovered that when you open the back door even a chink into the world of darkness, the darkness soon comes flooding back.

On the night of the attack, Jack got a phone call in the middle of the night. A young Christian lad called Phil was staying with them overnight. Phil had completed a rehab programme and had become friends with the couple. He was attending the Greenock branch of the church. The phone call was from a friend of Gerry's, letting Jack and Jenny know that Gerry had been attacked and was in the hospital. When Jack found out the details of who was involved, he was of one mindset: he was angry! Phil decided to pack his bags and stay elsewhere that night.

Unfortunately, one wrong choice on Jack's part led to many, and before too long, he and Jenny found their faith slipping away. Sadly, they didn't reappear at church for three or four years and soon returned to their old ways. He described it, on reflection, as a gradual process of wrong choices: like going down a set of stairs, and you suddenly find yourself at the bottom.

He found it easy to backslide. He had made the mistake of leaving a back door open to his old life by leaving the phone numbers of all his contacts on his mobile. He quickly began to phone around them and arranged to meet them at one of the drug dens. Jack was hoping that those responsible for the attack on Gerry would be there, but, fortunately for him, they were not there. He soon heard the whole story of those who had attacked his son, and of course, being amongst old friends again, he became determined to pursue them: Jack soon had the situation under control.

Now Jack was back in touch with the wrong kind of people. Soon he was back into his old habits of taking drugs. And now, not only was he taking drugs but dealing again. By this time a new street drug called Valium was out, sold in blister packs. Jack would buy a few thousand at a time and started making money again, selling them on the street. The night of Gerry's attack was the return of three long, dark years away from God. Jack said these years were worse than his earlier years as he was no longer ignorant of the way of salvation. He had experienced forgiveness and peace and knew this was taking him further away into the old familiar darkness. It was not the right road for him.

During this time, Jack's past caught up with him. He ended up in jail again, this time for six months for an earlier crime, fraud. While in jail, Jack began to go through withdrawal symptoms as he came off alcohol and drugs. He found himself in a dark place mentally and physically. The prison officers put him in isolation for nine days for safety. Jack believed that the officers thought they would take him away to a mental hospital because he appeared to be losing his mind, but he pulled through these dark, difficult days. As he began to recover from his withdrawals, he discovered he had time to stop and reflect. He used the time to get his house in order. He attempted to pray and sing when on his own, and he soon felt God speaking to him to return to Him again. This was an opportunity not only to break free from drugs but also to seek God. On several occasions he was accused of singing Jesus songs, Christian choruses, by other prisoners! Jack said there was a big guy Jeremy who used to walk into his cell, who used to tease him again and again when he found him singing the songs that he had learned at church. Other things helped him too. Graham, my husband, wrote him a letter, and as he read it, he became very aware of the draw on his spirit to return to God again. This was particularly significant for Jack because Graham was a retired police officer who spoke kindly to him about his backslidings. Jack began to pray more often when other notes arrived from Billy, another church contact. Something was starting to change inside him.

However, Jack was not only needing encouragement

from his church family; he needed a miracle, an intervention from God. Unfortunately, as soon as he was released from prison, the things of God were quickly forgotten, and he returned to his old way of life. But Christ was pursuing Jack's soul; the work that started in prison was not in vain. It was not long before things began to improve.

Whilst Jack had been inside, the church continued to pray for the couple, even though we did not know any details, and we certainly had no idea that he had been in prison! Jack and Jenny never seemed very far away from our hearts, and we were often prompted by little incidents that, looking back now, we can see were of some significance.

One of these was when Pauline, a faithful church member and taxi driver, was on a taxi run in Coatbridge. She just happened to be dropping someone off near Jenny's home and spotted Jenny across the road. Pauline went over to speak to her, inviting her to return to church. Jenny was unsure about returning; folks generally didn't know Jack was in jail, but she agreed to try it as a one-off the following Sunday night. She had been through a difficult time. Whilst Jack had been in isolation she had had no contact with him because he was too ill to communicate. Although he was no longer in isolation and was beginning to recover from his withdrawals, she was still worried about his health. Shortly after meeting Jenny, Pauline shared with us at our next church meeting how she had met Jenny and asked us to increase our prayers, although she didn't mention any of the details to the congregation. This certainly encouraged us to pray.

Meanwhile, everything seemed to stop Jenny from coming along that Sunday night. After visiting Jack in jail that afternoon, she got a flat tyre on the way to church. She felt she could not break her promise to Pauline, so after phoning a family friend who came and changed the tyre, she arrived at church half an hour late. Jenny said she would never forget that visit because as she walked in, we all stopped listening to the sermon and all clapped with delight at seeing her, including the preacher! There was such a genuine love for her that it was an outburst of spontaneous happiness seeing one of our former church family members returning. Jenny said she just felt straightaway, "I'm home."

Later, in her own words, she said, "We didn't know you were all praying for us when Jack was in jail; that was God and the power of prayer that brought us back."

On another occasion, not long after Jack was out of jail, but before the couple returned to the church, Billy popped around to visit. Jenny was in the middle of leaving the house with her belongings. Jack was going through a difficult time; Jenny had had enough! She could never put up with his nonsense for very long! Some wives might learn a lesson or two from Jenny! With her belongings tied up in a couple of bin bags, she walked past Billy, telling him in no uncertain terms not to go into the house. Billy ignored her and went in anyway to discover Jack covered in blood.

Bit by bit, God was performing His unseen miracle in Jack's heart. He had an old pal Jo who was coming around to the house from time to time. The two men would sit up late chatting and taking Valium together. On one of these occasions, Jack found himself telling Jo about God and the good old days at church. Before long, he had invited Jo to church. Jo was keen to come and hear about God. Suddenly, Jack had a good reason to return!

But before they did, Graham and I dropped by to visit them on the off chance they would be in. Jack saw us through the glass front door walking up the garden path and ran upstairs to avoid embarrassment. As we knocked, we could see his form disappearing at top speed upstairs! At that time, they had a dog called Tyson. My memory is of a wee yappy dog that I was wary of as he just might nip my ankles! I was very unsure of him! I walked in and laughingly told Jenny to get the dog upstairs and get Jack downstairs! Jack appeared after a few minutes, laughing sheepishly about his behaviour. He now admits he was embarrassed and frightened of the spiritual part of me.

Soon their mistakes and failures turned into joy as Jack and Jenny returned to the church and began again to find their way into the presence of God. They soon discovered their former joy restored as they found forgiveness from their backsliding.

Jack returned first, accompanied by his pal Jo. Although Jenny had received such a warm welcome when she visited the church that Sunday evening, she didn't return for a while. She admits now that she would have loved to but did not want to return and leave again. She waited to see if Jack's decision to return to church was a genuine commitment this time. On reflection, Jenny hesitated because she had been let down so often; she was afraid to put her hope in this new way of life again. However, Jack was determined that things would be different now. He understood what a Christian was and knew he truly wanted this Christian lifestyle and commitment to God. He found a place of deep repentance and peace again. This time, he began absorbing more teaching, participating in church services, raising his hands in worship, and praying. The whole service took on a new meaning for him. As Jenny realised how determined and genuine Jack was, she was encouraged and began to attend church meetings too. They were given a warm welcome and were very glad to be back again with us.

The couple was restored fully in their faith. They had learned much from their mistakes when they were away from the church. One thing they knew now was that they genuinely wanted this new way of life and did not want the old darkness anymore. They became determined to set themselves to follow God's ways.

However, even after Jack had been a consistent member of our church for a good number of years, and despite the changes in his life, he still managed to get into bother with the police! By this time we knew him well and heard about the incident from Jack himself. He eventually managed to see the funny side of it! It involved someone the family knew, who not only phoned the police but came to his house on one occasion when very distressed and accused Jack of all sorts of falsities. Jack ended up in the back of a police van, cuffed and taken down to the station for questioning! I must say he was never charged, and although he found the whole incident rather humiliating at the time, in later years he developed a good working relationship with the police.

13 Cemented Faith

Jack realised that this time around, his understanding of church was different. He was now listening carefully and learning new things. He knew and had experienced the strong presence of God, but he found some of the truths in the Bible difficult to understand. His head was full of questions, and he had no answers. He realised he needed to absorb the teaching and put it into practice. He found it hard to understand some fundamental concepts: the Crucifixion, the Resurrection, the Trinity, and the Virgin birth. Again, God came and helped him not only to accept these fundamental truths of the Christian faith but to understand them. He said, "I came to the church when I was 51 and knew nothing about spiritual things. Even though I got saved, I still had a lot of doubts." It was like a jigsaw that he couldn't fit together to see the complete picture.

He remembered walking into the Cumbernauld church with wee Billy. In his head, he was puzzling over the Trinity and turned to Billy and asked, 'Which one do you call Lord?' Billy was always short with his explanations! Looking straight at Jack, he said, "The one in the middle. He died for you!"[30]

Sitting in his living room one evening, Jack tried to grasp something of the truth about the Cross. As he puzzled

---

[30] We would not necessarily agree with Billy over this! The Godhead and the Trinity are all the same Divine Being. In Luke's Gospel 3:21 and 22, we read that as Jesus was baptised in water, the Holy Spirit descended on Him, and a voice from heaven said: 'You are my Son.' This verse demonstrates that God the Father, Son and Holy Spirit are united. Therefore the answer to Jack's question should have been, 'All of them.'

over it, he switched on his tablet to find a sermon. He listened intently, and Christ came to him. In a moment, he found a belief that entered his soul, and he suddenly understood the fundamental truth that Christ had died for him. He explained that is when he believed. He did not accept it because of a church or the minister's prayers but because God Himself had come to him when he was alone. Later that evening, Billy phoned him, asking how he was doing. Excitement flooded over Jack as he began to speak to him about what had been revealed in his spirit. Jack said to Billy at the time, "It was like a vision that had come to me. Jesus was revealing Himself to me. It was just beautiful."

Another difficulty Jack had was trying to work out the Trinity: how Jesus was related to God, how they could be one person and who was the Holy Spirit. After he came home from a Saturday night meeting in our Glasgow branch, he felt confused; he couldn't work it out and put it all together. The whole Father and Son relationship was a total puzzle to him. By attending church regularly and listening carefully to the preaching, he began to understand that God the Father, God the Son and God the Holy Spirit were all one. When he realised that Christ was God; and the Holy Spirit was God too, it all just made complete sense. He said, "My thoughts began to come into the fold." Jack started to build on that foundation, learning what he could as he grasped the reality of the knowledge that Christ was his Saviour and had died for him. He realised that one of the reasons his faith was not strong in those first two years was because, in his mind, it had all been about God. He had never really built a relationship with Jesus. He can remember moments in church when the truth dawned on him. He said, "On one occasion, I was listening to someone speaking about Solomon, and they mentioned, 'He was the wisest man that ever lived, apart from Jesus of course, because *He* was God'". This opened Jack's eyes, and he started appreciating how wise and perfect Christ was. It was these throwaway comments that helped him to piece things together. This led him to search for a closer relationship with God.

As Jack continued to search, he threw himself more on God in prayer. He didn't discuss his thoughts with other family members because, in the past, he had always tried to keep his troubles to himself. Now that he was in the church, he never discussed his unbelief and doubts with Jenny. She had a church background and was sent to Sunday School as a child, so she had never had difficulty accepting these fundamental truths. Jack realised that it was just the way he had to learn, by himself.

Again, he can remember when the revelation came to him concerning the Resurrection. He was not long out of prison and had been thinking about the things of God. He searched on his tablet for a sermon about Jesus. This time he found one about the Resurrection; everything that he knew and understood about Christ started fitting together and made complete sense, and with that came the ability to accept the teachings about Christ, believe He was the Son of God and have faith that He had risen from the dead. Although he had never succeeded in anything when he went to school, he studied the Bible with the help of a concordance. He made notes until it all became clear to him. He finally saw the plan of God for the salvation of man. He understood something of the Trinity, the Cross and the Resurrection. It was as if he suddenly saw the complete picture. Describing it to me, he said, "I just felt wow! And I mean, wow!"

When I asked Jack what cemented his faith, his answer was clear and concise. "God revealed Himself to me on the night of the 6th of February 2014." A mind-blowing statement for an ex-drug addict, alcoholic and criminal!

He described it thus:

"There had been a growing ache inside me to know God better. So, it was a Friday night, and I had been walking around the park with Tyson, my late mother's dog, and I found within myself a cry like a prayer going up to heaven: God, reveal yourself to me."

He laughed later, saying that he had never used the word reveal before in his whole life! He was grateful for the level of understanding he had found in his search for God, but he knew he needed more than just head knowledge. He needed to be filled. As he walked around the park, he used a Walkman that David, another church friend, had given him. Jack played songs whilst praying to God; he could feel a fire in his belly, and even though he was in a public park, his hands were raised as he sought God. The ache continued when he got home. In his living room, he attempted to write a letter to his nephew, who was in prison at the time, whilst Jenny was sitting on the other couch reading her Bible. He started playing a song that touched a chord within him: 'Holy Spirit, how I love you.' He kept on playing it over and over again even though he didn't know very much about the Holy Spirit. Jenny had left the room at some point and gone upstairs, and suddenly he was overwhelmed with the power and presence of God. He described it as waves going right over him down to his feet. He fell to his knees and worshipped. He said, "It was so beautiful, I will never forget it. It was the most beautiful experience that had ever happened to me. I ended up on my knees in my living room. It was as if God revealed Himself to me in such a way that He said, "'I know all these doubts you've got. Jack, here I am.'"

He went upstairs to tell Jenny; he couldn't even raise his voice but could only speak in a hushed whisper. He then returned downstairs and again fell on his knees by his chair, absorbing the presence for several hours. The impact of that encounter was such that he lay awake half the night.

In Jack's own words, "Honestly, I don't exaggerate it one bit. I'd say I'm underplaying it the way I'm trying to describe it: it was phenomenal and beautiful. If ever I get any rocky spiritual feelings, God always reminds me of that time. I could hardly walk, in fact, I couldn't get up at one point. It was beautiful, even my voice was soft. There was no medication, nothing. I've had highs and lows, but I've never experienced anything like this in my life. I've never had it since then. I've had lots of blessings in church but never like that! That was enough; you couldn't live there, could you? You'd just fall aff! It was beautiful, that's how good it is."

Jenny joined in the conversation, explaining that he was particularly hungry for God at that time. He was reading his Bible and watching sermons from various people, such as Billy Graham. He had been seeking for several days, and that Friday night had a wonderful experience.

She had gone to bed and heard him coming up. After years of living with an addict, her initial reaction when she saw him was that Jack was high on something! However, he hadn't been taking anything for a long time, so she knew he couldn't be; he had left that old lifestyle behind long ago, and besides that, he hadn't met up with any old friends. She described Jack as "just standing at the bedroom door, with an expression of wonder on his face, which was all aglow. He was starry-eyed."

Even as he talked about it again, his face began to grow radiant with the memory of the presence of God. His voice softened as he reflected on that wonderful touch of God. He said it left him speechless; he would never forget it. He explained, "It's a place you couldn't live in. That's how beautiful it was." Jenny exclaimed that she wished she could live there. We smiled, reassuring her that one day she would!

Later, Jack used a song called 'Pour over me" to describe what he had felt on that occasion: as if the Holy Spirit was pouring over him and deep down inside him. This experience only happened once, although he had had many blessings in the church. It was an encounter with God.

He tried telling wee Billy about it. Billy summarised it by saying, "He touched you." Jack laughed; it was as if his pal was saying to him, "Aye, all right!"

Since then, Jack has had his ups and downs but has never returned to the old life of violence, drugs, and drinking. Something about the spiritual world had become incredibly real to him. Even though there were unknown battles ahead, Jack never wavered again.

He discovered after that experience that he would wake up every morning at 3 a.m. as if an inner alarm clock woke him, and he would sit on the stairs in the family home and read and pray. He found his faith cemented, and his beliefs became certainties within himself.

He explained that he has never been very good at quoting verses, but there is one verse that sticks with him all the time:

'Trust in the Lord with all your heart and lean not on your own understanding' (Proverbs 3:5).

Jack tried to keep spiritual things as simple as he could. He discovered he ran into problems when he started to work things out for himself. I asked him if he would like to be further along the spiritual road, and his response was simple. He said, "Of course I would! But am I happy with what God has done for me? Of course I am, and I know it's got nothing to do with me, and I now know it's all God. What he has given me is peace. I can sum it up in one word: peace – a good night's sleep! Years ago, that was unknown, but now I have peace. He makes you accountable to your family and God, number one."

Lots of things began to change: Jack and Jenny started reading the Bible as a couple and discussing the parts they didn't understand, a house group was held in their home, and they loved the fellowship and togetherness that brought. Not only that, but an incredible thirst laid hold of Jack, not a physical thirst this time, but a thirst for the things of God. The more he learned, the more amazed he was, and then the more he wanted to know.

As Jack began to find Christ for himself, he was able to describe it:

"For me, you begin to look to see what kind of man Christ is, and you realise how perfect He is. Everything is perfect about Him – love, kindness, everything was good about Him, and you want to emulate that. He is the greatest Man that ever lived on the face of the Earth! And when you begin to understand that, it's phenomenal. No matter what struggles we get in life or death, whatever struggles, He died to give me freedom. You just begin to open your eyes and realise what He's done."

His favourite book in the Bible is the Gospel of John, where he learned about Christ being a man. He loved reading the parables Jesus told, and marvelled at His wisdom when dealing with others. The Gospel of John is the first book Jack turned to. He loves to absorb the truth about Christ. "I read, I pause, and then I write down the bit I want to remember," he said.

Jack got himself into a routine with church. He loved a Sunday morning communion service. There were times when he first started coming when he felt perplexed because it was as if the preacher was reading the thoughts in his head! He said that happened less now, but he felt very settled and at home in church with his church family. Being blessed brings contentment.

He discovered that to maintain this spiritual glow he had found, he had to be very careful.

This was vital: he lived in the danger zone's heart: Coatbridge was and still is renowned for its drug problem. This area, known as the Monkland District, has the third-highest total of deaths in Scotland. It is at the heart of a drug-related death epidemic and is described as in drug crisis.

So although he was finding deep contentment and peace in God, the devil at times could be very near, and Jack learned the vital lesson of keeping his guard up and a watchful eye for the enemy of souls at all times.

He commented on the importance of the choice of friendships. He said, "It's nice to be about the right kind of people." Jack had learned that even though he had been on the right road for some time, the temptation was never far away. The wrong kind of company affects our choices, and he discovered that he had to work to keep himself right.

He gave an example of something that happened as he learned to walk in Christ. He was walking with his little grandson when he saw an old acquaintance, whom he hadn't seen for years, coming towards him across the park. It was someone that Jack used to work with within the drug world. After the initial conversation, he was offered drugs, but he quickly explained that he was now going to church and did not want drugs. The guy knew Jack was going to church, but he was still going to try to persuade him, offering him this or that, telling him that, after all, he was a churchgoer too, or at least went around the different churches; so it would be okay for one like himself to take drugs! He continued to try and persuade Jack by making suggestions of how much money he could be bringing home. When money is short, this can be a big temptation: it was the exact issue that Jack had fallen on all these years ago when he had a young family and began getting involved in the drug scene. He held firm, looked him straight in the eye and said, "Money can't buy what I have found." However, his so-called friend continued to pressurise him and eventually, they swapped phone numbers.

After a while, he managed to get away and came home. He was alarmed at how quickly the tempter had drawn near and how troubled he was in his spirit. After all, he thought, he could do with a bit more money. Thankfully, Jack shut the door firmly to any insinuations that might come to him. He was learning how to fight the devil with the wisdom he so admired in his Lord, and he turned to seek help from his Bible. He came across this verse and not only applied the first part to himself but sent it to his old friend:

> "If this is so, then the Lord knows how to rescue the godly from trials and to hold the unrighteous for punishment on the day of judgment" (2 Peter 2:9 NIVUK).

After sending the text, Jack deleted the man's mobile number. He knew he had to keep himself firmly fixed on Christ; he made it clear that he wasn't interested in getting involved again.

He learned to watch out for these sneaky temptations that came in the back door when he least expected them. When he first began to attend the church, he was claiming benefits that he shouldn't have been. That crime eventually caught up with him, and he spent time in prison for fraud. Now, he knew he was accountable to God and his family. He sums it up very nicely in his own words:

"I just remove myself from the streets now. It's not that I judge them, but I know they're not good for me. If I associate myself with the people I once knew then I'm going to go down the same hole! Now, I have no contact with them – their numbers are not on my phone anymore. I'm not interested in going down the wrong road, but instead I surround myself with godly people and I'm happy being quiet."

He learned the importance of making the right choices inside and outside his home. He found that violence and sexual filth on television disgusted him. He said, "I used to think I couldn't live without a TV, and now I'd rather it was off." Again and again, he found himself turning to Jenny and suggesting they put the television off or at least watch something better. She agreed with him. Only God can bring these changes within us: that's the miracle!

As they have continued to listen to God, both have grown spiritually. Jenny spoke of something recently that made me feel she had grasped the spiritual concept of having a clear spirit before God.

It was a glorious, hot sunny day last summer, and the couple decided to go away for the day to the beach. They were sitting watching the kids playing, but as they did, they were aware that they were growing increasingly uncomfortable with the scene that they were watching.

They felt shocked at what they now know to be sin: older women in their 30s and 40s drunk on the beach, shouting and swearing and wearing scanty swimwear. It wasn't a happy scene. Even though they hadn't done anything wrong, they felt the scene shadowed their spirits. Jenny explained that this particular spot used to be full of happy childhood memories where her family would often come, and yet now, she was so changed that she was aware of the sin in others that once she had known herself.

Now, no one was sitting telling Jenny and Jack these things. As they had been learning to abide more deeply in Him, they had been taught directly by the Holy Spirit. Christ had become their home; they saw their old ways in a new light. It made them realise how far they had come. In the Bible, the book of Lamentations 4:1, describes the shadow of sin like tarnished gold. This relates to the way Jenny and Jack felt. It wasn't that they had deliberately chosen to sin, but they found their spirits dull after being in a particular atmosphere. It demonstrated to them just how carefully they needed to live to preserve the clear shining of the presence and power of Christ in their hearts.

How good it was for the couple to recognise that when they had lost their shine, they could pray to God and get right with Him again by coming to the Cross and finding fresh cleansing.

14 Deeper Conflict and Victory

And so their story is brought almost right up to date. During the Coronavirus pandemic, Jack and Jenny spent much of their time in lockdown, sitting out in their garden with their Bibles and books, enjoying reading together. They were progressively working their way through the Bible and discussing the parts they did not understand.

As we visited them on one occasion and sat together in their living room, Jack described how he felt: "This gives you an idea of where God has brought us. Honestly, I sit here in the peace and quiet of God and it's just, oh, perfect." The couple had found contentment in the great peace of God. Jack often reflected on the happiness that was now in their home. He thought the only reason Jenny was still with him was because of God. She used to say, 'Jack, I love you, but I can't live with you.' God changed that! There were many times in the past when Jenny had had to leave home, but now she says: "Our marriage is the best it has ever been." In almost fifty years of married life, Jenny and Jack had never known such a stable relationship – a peace and strength that has been unique for them. She said with a twinkle in her eye on one of these occasions, "I knew there was always a good person in there, it was just getting him out! We've been married 46 years; if we get another four years, then we'll have our golden [wedding anniversary]."

But there were further trials ahead that the couple knew nothing about. More recently, they had to face something which every parent dreads – the death of a child. They lost their beloved Gerry through a tragic accident, and although they have been shaken to the very core of what and who they are, they have remained faithful to Christ through it all. They have marvelled at His keeping power and cannot even begin to imagine how they would have coped without the One who has been their helper and support.

It was all very sudden and tragic. Gerry, who was in his thirties, was in difficulties. He had been using drugs for years, which had affected his physical and mental health. The tragic incident happened like this. He had been visiting his parents one morning. Jack had been out in the garden, working in his shed, when his son came out for a chat and asked to borrow twenty pounds, but Jack did not have any cash to give him. Gerry turned to his Dad and said, "Never mind." He smiled cheerily and, as he left, shouted upstairs to his Mum, "Bye, love you," as he always did. Then he turned to his Dad and said, "See you later," but there was no later. He was found unconscious within an hour and a half of leaving their home, having taken drugs that appeared to be from a bad batch. Gerry was rushed to the local hospital but never again regained consciousness and died days later.

It was the biggest challenge that Jack and Jenny have ever faced, but the difference now from earlier years was that neither of them let go of their faith. Instead, they held on to God and found His strength. Jack said that, again and again, he was reminded of these earlier touches from God in his own home. The sweet memories of the presence of God held them when they were broken, and it seemed everything had been taken from them. They had found the Rock and were both holding fast.

In his own words, "You keep yourself right on the small things, and God keeps you right on the big. Even the night Gerry passed away I just felt the presence of God all around. The night we were saying our goodbyes to Gerry would've been a whole different scenario if we hadn't been attending church. We had the song "Immanuel" playing,[31] and we were calm and at peace. We were whispering to him, saying 'God is waiting on you.' God was all around us, and it was beautiful."

Jack was touched by the kindness and compassion of the nurses who worked in the ward Gerry was in. He thought one of them must have been a Christian as she came over and, despite the pandemic, put her arms around Jack and said, "It doesn't seem like it now, but God will get you through it."

There were so many rumours that were going around the neighbourhood concerning Gerry's death. The drug dealers had fled the scene and taken refuge down south, the police were involved, and well-wishers came to visit Jack and Jenny to share their version of events, but none added up. It was a difficult time for the couple, but God helped them and gave them strength in the situation, and they learned to close their ears to the lies of seeming 'do-gooders'.

The couple had always said that if something happened to one of their kids, they didn't know how they would manage or what they would do. What they found they did was that they relied and leaned heavily on God in the most awful of circumstances.

---

[31] "Immanuel" by Michael Card.

In Jenny's own words, "We've just given it all to God, and that's the reason we are sitting here today. Otherwise, if we hadn't been to church, and we hadn't found God, if we hadn't been walking the right way, I don't know where we would be. God has been here with us every step of the way. He has kept us strong and at peace. If Jack had still been drinking when that happened to Gerry, he would have ended up in jail for a long, long time, or been dead by now. The anger that would have been in him, if he wasn't following God's path, would have been uncontrollable."

And Jack said, "Don't get me wrong I can still get angry: that's one thing I need to work on. But see, when that thing happened to Gerry ... and all the different stories we heard from different people telling us how he had died ... if I hadn't been strong enough spiritually with Christ's strength, I probably would be in jail by now! There was a time when I wouldn't have listened to God, being the stubborn kind of person I was, but I know I'm not that person anymore. Sometimes I believe God takes things away, and I find myself saying double WOW! There was a boy in here (Jack's home) yesterday who was telling me about Gerry's death, and he was swearing like a trooper. Sometimes you can be up to your knees in blood and thunder and you don't want to listen to it anymore. Even our kids when they come into the house and they slip up swearing, they apologise to us, and they know I used to have a tongue that could cut steel!"

Jenny talked about the reassurance of peace she felt surrounding Gerry's death. One night in distress, she turned to God and found an indescribable peace coming over her in waves. The wonderful reassurance washed over her from heaven above that Gerry, who had once committed to Christ, was safe in His arms now. All the mental torture he had experienced at the end of his life was now over. The presence was so strong she could never deny it.

The funeral that followed was small due to Covid restrictions, but it was watched online by over 21,000 viewers. Gerry and his family are widely known in the Coatbridge area. Jenny spoke of the peace that held her. She stood at the open grave as the coffin was lowered and said, "I felt God all around me, and I felt He gave me the strength to cope."

That day was so different from the one she had dreaded. It is still hard for them both, but they are learning day by day and moment by moment to lean on Him. They can only imagine what life would have been like without God. They found the poem *Footprints* very relevant to their situation. When they were too numb to feel God's presence, they were reassured that He was carrying them.

The couple were honest and said they found it hard to get back to reading their Bibles straightaway after Gerry's death. They prayed hard but found it difficult to read.

More recently, Jack spoke of listening to the audible Bible. He has now been diagnosed with early-onset dementia and finds reading difficult: words become muddled on a page. Sometimes he still reads and makes notes, but he finds listening easier. Jack explained that the daily readings from his Bible verses are strengthening and helpful.

The profound experience of the presence of God that he had had at home several years earlier made Jenny wonder if God was preparing them for something. She had often pondered whether there was a storm ahead. She realised now that Jack needed the memory of that experience and the strength it gave him to hold on through the worst time of their life. Both of them commented on the fact that God gives you enough to cope. She spoke of finding Christ anew a few Sundays after Gerry's funeral. Although the congregation had just returned to the physical church building after a year of lockdown, at that point the couple had not ventured out to church. As Jenny listened to the church service online in the quietness of her own home, she felt it was as if God was putting a big blanket of love around her, comforting, and protecting her. "It was beautiful, like floating on clouds, like a big fluffy blanket around me, I just felt dead[32] at peace. I believe He does give you something to hang onto in the bad times."

Whenever Jack feels a bit low about his health, he is reminded of that moment in his living room that changed his life forever. The beauty of Christ comes over him each time he thinks or talks about it.

The couple believes that all the trials they have faced, and the blessings they have been given, have prepared them for events like the passing of Gerry. The verse "I can do all things through Christ who strengthens me" (Philippians 4:13 NKJV) has meant so much to Jack throughout the years. Whenever faced with a difficulty, he would read it aloud to himself, convincing himself of the

---

[32] Scottish slang. Meaning 'very' – enhances the meaning of the phrase.

power of the words. This verse is now on the wall in their home. He said, "I just keep looking at that verse and believing in it. I say to God, 'I can get through this with your help and with your strength.' I understand that now. During the first two years of being a Christian, I thought I was doing well being off the drink and drugs. I thought that I had arrived; I was doing so well. But now I realise it is all God, He holds us and keeps us through it all. I know I could fall like that [Jack snapped his fingers] if I turned the wrong way. Temptation is cunning, baffling, and powerful. It'll kid you on and then take you down."

Interestingly, after their brother's tragic death, Jack's children thought that Dad would go back to drinking again. His daughter Alison was worried, but Jenny knew Jack would hold on, knowing how real his faith had become to him. When Jenny told him of their worries, Jack was surprised! He said that if he had fallen, he would have done it long before this occasion!

Over the following months, Jack and Jenny learned to cope with the death of their son. They have returned to the church and are participating in the services again. Life will never be quite the same as before, but their faith is strong. They have faced their worst fears and have experienced first-hand how God can help, comfort and support them in a crisis. God has brought them safely through these tragic circumstances. He will keep them through the rest of their lives. They are unsure what is ahead with Jack's diagnosis of dementia. Along with the church, they are making this a matter of prayer.

I asked Jack to finish by talking about some of his intimate experiences with Christ.

"If you got that every week, you'd be like ecstatic!" he said laughingly, waving his hands high over his head. "A one-off is enough. It was beautiful, although I'd love another one! It's a wonderful thing when you begin to understand the things of God. I understand Him in my own way, and I just love it. Would I love to be more spiritual? I am over the moon with where God has brought me. I am content and at peace with myself. That's what people are searching for when they try drink and drugs. There is a contentment that you get, it's spiritual, and it's just lovely."

We give God glory that He has brought Jack and Jenny thus far and will guide them the rest of the way until they lay their crowns at His feet, lost in the sheer wonder of salvation, forgiven, and deeply loved and accepted by God.

Note to Readers

If you would like to know more about Christian teaching and the action of Christ in lives today, further reading is suggested in the list of books below, written by one of the founders of Struthers Memorial Group of Churches. Contact details are provided in the book order form at the end.

It may also be of interest to know that Struthers currently runs three conferences in Scotland each year – New Year, Easter and August, and one in Wales in May. Friends gather from many parts of Britain. An open invitation is extended to all and particularly to those interested in the baptism in the Holy Spirit and related themes. Details will be provided on enquiry at the New Dawn Bookshop, Greenock (contact details below).

Books by Hugh Black

The Baptism in the Spirit and Its Effects

Used in bringing people into the baptism in the Spirit and described as one of the clearest, most incisive books on the subject. This expanded edition includes evidence that Finney, Moody and Spurgeon spoke in tongues, and narrates miraculous effects of the baptism in the lives of two individuals.

Reflections on the Gifts of the Spirit

Deals in an original way with its subject. The chapters on miracles, healings and discernment (with deliverance) have roused great interest and led to positive action. Anecdotes and illustrations have been much appreciated.

Reflections on a Song of Love

A highly original commentary on 1 Corinthians 13. The drawing power of love pervades this fascinating study. The author shows very clearly how this chapter fully supports and in no way detracts from the doctrine of Pentecost.

A Trumpet Call to Women

Presents a strong case from Scripture for greater involvement of women in ministry. It throws much light on those portions which on the surface seem to put women in a subject role. It includes the testimony of Elizabeth H. Taylor, a lady much used of God. A stirring book, demanding a response – a call to action.

Consider Him

Considers a number of the qualities of Christ. He Himself seems to speak from the pages of the book, both in the main text and in the testimony of Jennifer Jack, whose selfless presentation truly leaves the reader to consider Christ.

Battle for the Body

It will take courage to face the truths highlighted in this original approach to fundamental issues of sanctification. The second part presents the powerful testimony of John Hamilton – a preacher widely known and loved.

The Clash of Tongues: With Glimpses of Revival

Part One is a commentary on 1 Corinthians 14. It deals in detail with some of the more difficult questions. Part Two deals with the relationship between revival and Pentecost and refers to the 1939 and 1949 revivals in Lewis, introducing a number of people who were involved in the first of these – particularly Mary MacLean, whose remarkable testimony is related. This book may particularly appeal to people studiously inclined.

The Incomparable Christ

Part One deals with the gospel. It faces honestly the questions of Christ's resurrection and that of all men. It deals in a direct way with the doctrine of hell and eternal judgment, and gives practical instruction on the way of salvation. Part Two presents the remarkable testimonies of two young women.

Gospel Vignettes

Focuses attention on various facets of the gospel, with chapter titles such as: Ye Must Be Born Again, The Life-Giving Water, Weighed in the Balances, Behold I Stand at the Door and Knock, The Hour of Decision. Includes testimonies of three people whose lives have been transformed by Christ, to one of whom Christ Himself appeared. One of these testimonies is from Diana Rutherford, the author of Jacko. Useful in the gospel, but introducing the pentecostal dimension.

Reflections from Abraham

Outlines spiritual principles seen in the life of Abraham. It deals with his call and ours, the mountain as distinct from the valley life, intercession, Lot in Sodom, the sacrifice of Isaac and the way of faith. Part Two tells of the action of God in the life of Dorothy Jennings, to whom Abraham was of particular significance.

Reflections from Moses:
With the Testimony of Dan McVicar

Part One shows the outworking of spiritual principles such as the calling and training of a man of God, the need to start from holy ground, deliverance from bondage, and the consequences of Moses' failure in a critical hour. Part Two presents the late well-known evangelist Dan McVicar's story in his own words. The conversion of this militant communist and the intervention of God in the lives of his parents make thrilling reading.

Christ the Deliverer

Deals with both physical and spiritual deliverance. It includes a number of remarkable testimonies to healing, e.g. from blindness, manic depression, ME, rheumatoid arthritis, spinal injury, phobias, nightmares. It speaks of the appearance of angels, touches on revival and analyses the theory of 'visualization'.

Christian Fundamentals

Part One deals with the individual and his needs in the realms of salvation, baptism in the Spirit, and deliverance. Testimonies include that of the author's daughter Mary Black. Part Two focuses on the outflow of the life of God to meet the needs of others through vocal, hidden and open power ministries. The end times are the subject of Part Three.

Reflections from David

This searching book shows a man after God's own heart in the glory of his achievements and the tragedy of his failings. Divine retribution and forgiveness, the joy of deliverance, and the action of God in present-day lives are all examined.

Pioneers of the Spiritual Way

From a lost Eden our race walked a lost road, occasionally experiencing higher things as pioneers of the spiritual way led upwards. The impassable barrier between God and man was finally removed as the last Adam blasted a way through: Christ, bringing many sons to glory.

Revival:
Including the Prophetic Vision of Jean Darnall

Some of the great revivals of the past are reviewed with their enduring principles and changing patterns. Revival comes nearer as we are confronted with more recent movements of God. The celebrated vision of Jean Darnall has left many with a feeling of keen expectation for coming days.

Revival: Personal Encounters

From the treasure chest of memory the author brings a series of revival-related incidents. We hear of Studd, Burton and Salter and of revival in the Congo and Rwanda. More is revealed of the moving of God in Lewis and at an unusual Scottish school camp. A contemporary scene in Brazil brings revival very close. 'The highly original testimony of Alison Speirs brings the fact and challenge right to our doorstep.

Revival: Living in the Realities

For a revived or a revival-conscious people a high level of Christian living is immediately presented. The experience of revival has to be outworked. This book ponders issues such as spiritual warfare, what it means to be imitators of Christ, the need to progress from forgiveness to love for those who do us harm, and the mystery of the love of God itself. An unusual and thought-provoking book.

E. H. Taylor, A Modern Christian Mystic:
Sayings and Recollections (ed. by Hugh Black)

The sequel to *A Trumpet Call to Women*, this highly unusual book contains insights into a wide range of spiritual themes on the part of one who was much used in predictive prophecy and in leading people into the baptism in the Spirit and deliverance, and especially into a deep knowledge of Christ.

War in Heaven and Earth

This book illuminates the subject of spiritual warfare both at the 'ground level' of day-to-day living where the devil's weapons are met with the weapons of Christ, and at the unseen level of conflict where the power of Christ breaks the hold of spiritual entities over specific territorial areas.

A View from the Floor

What happens when the power of the Holy Spirit comes upon someone? The first of a series, this book of testimonies traces the effects of a spiritual movement which began in November 1994 and continues to the present time. It is fascinating to learn some of the detail of what happens when we find ourselves on God's operating table.

Further Views from the Floor
(co-author: A. H. Black)

Weeping, laughing, singing, dancing ... whatever is happening in the Church? This book attempts through many personal testimonies to probe beneath the surface of the external manifestations. It strikingly portrays the reality of a Christ-centred revelation of God to lives in need or simply desiring to know more of Him.

Evidence from the Floor
(co-author: A. H. Black)
Whether it be in healing from a spider phobia or revival in Mexico, the living Christ is manifested wherever He finds responsive hearts. Wonderful experiences 'on the floor' are told here at first hand. Of particular significance are Kenny Borthwick's visions of the lion-soul of Scotland and of coming revival.

Till I See You Clearly
(Co-author: A. H. Black)
Times of difficulty can prompt us to question God's role in our lives. In answer, find the strong encouragement that this book offers as it takes us behind the scenes to look at:
- the dimension into which God wants to bring us
- the divine strategy in the life of Job
- inspiring testimonies of our own day

Forthcoming 2023:
Fire from the North:
Revival Reflections from Hugh Black
(Compiler and editor: John Caldwell, assisted by A. H. Black)
This is a daily devotional reader supplemented by contributions from Jean Darnall, Kenny Borthwick and Alison Speirs, all taken from Mr Black's published books. The reader is brought face to face with the reality and power of revival and will be encouraged to look expectantly to the One who ministers it to a waiting and willing people.

Book Orders

New Dawn Bookshop, 10A Jamaica Street, Greenock,
Renfrewshire, PA15 1XX, Scotland
Telephone 01475 729668   Fax 01475 728145
Website: www.struthers-church.org
Email: bookshop@struthers-church.org

ORDER FORM

Please send me books by Hugh B. Black indicated below:

Quantity	Title	Price
_____	The Baptism in the Spirit and Its Effects	£4.99
_____	Reflections on the Gifts of the Spirit	£2.75
_____	Reflections on a Song of Love (a commentary on 1 Corinthians 13)	£1.25
_____	A Trumpet Call to Women	£2.50

_____	Consider Him (Twelve Qualities of Christ)	£2.25
_____	Battle for the Body	£2.95
_____	The Clash of Tongues: With Glimpses of Revival	£2.75
_____	The Incomparable Christ	£2.75
_____	Gospel Vignettes	£2.95
_____	Reflections from Abraham	£2.50
_____	Reflections from Moses: With the Testimony of Dan McVicar	£2.99
_____	Christ the Deliverer	£2.99
_____	Christian Fundamentals	£3.50
_____	Reflections from David	£3.75

_____ Pioneers of the Spiritual Way   £4.99

_____ Revival: Including the Prophetic   £3.99
Vision of Jean Darnall

_____ Revival: Personal Encounters   £4.50

_____ Revival: Living in the Realities   £3.99

_____ E. H. Taylor: £4.50
A Modern Christian Mystic

_____ War in Heaven and Earth   £6.99

_____ A View from the Floor   £5.99

_____ Further Views from the Floor   £5.99

_____ The Evidence from the Floor   £6.99

_____ Till I See You Clearly   £5.99

_____ Fire from the North (forthcoming 2023)

Name . . . .

Address . . . .

. . . . Post Code . . . .

UK orders: please enclose payment including 90p p & p per book. Overseas orders: please pay on receipt (including postage at cost).